ATTACKING ZONE DEFENSES

Second Edition

John Kresse
Richard Jablonski

ISBN: 1-57167-047-5

Book Layout: Antonio J. Perez
Cover Design: Deborah M. Bellaire

Coaches Choice Books is an imprint of: Sagamore Publishing, Inc.
                                             P.O. Box 647
                                             Champaign, IL 61824-0647
                                             (217) 359-5940
                                             Fax: (217) 359-5975
                                             Web Site: http//www.sagamorepub.com

FOREWORD

One of the great joys of coaching basketball is the many people you meet and get to know through the game. I first got to know John Kresse when I was an assistant coach and he was a player under the legendary Joe Lapchick at St. John's University. I noticed the way this kid worked and the way he put time into the game. So I said to him, "Would you like to get involved in coaching?" That summer John went to Clair Bee's camp, which is the granddaddy of all camps, and I think that's where he really started to get involved.

John took his first job in 1964 at Christ the King High School in New York. A year later, when Coach Lapchick retired from St. John's and I was fortunate enough to succeed him, I asked John to join me as one of my assistants.

It's a great story. The first game I ever coached at St. John's was the freshmen against the varsity. John took the freshmen and beat me. He felt so bad he wouldn't come to practice the next day. That was the start of a long relationship. John was my assistant for the next 14 years—11 at St. John's and three with the New York Nets of the American Basketball Association. John left St. John's for Charleston in 1979 and has enjoyed great success there since that time.

It doesn't surprise me. You could tell at an early age that John was really a student of the game—that he had a certain flair. Sometimes you can develop that aspect in a person, but in John's case, you could see it was more than that. It was inherent.

You can see that John has a special "feel" for the game by the way he handles things. A lot of people can learn basketball from a book. But to be really successful you have to have a feel for the game. John has a great advantage because he's an excellent bench coach. He can change defenses very well. That's a gift. That's tough to teach. It has to be an inherent gift.

Besides that, John's whole life is dedicated to basketball. His love for the game is reflected in this book—a book which, in my opinion, provides a valuable resource for coaches at all levels.

Lou Carnesecca
Former Head Coach, St. John's University
1992 Inductee, Naismith Memorial Basketball Hall of Fame, Springfield, MA

How This Book Will Help Your Program

During more than three decades as a basketball coach I have seen a tremendous growth in the use and sophistication of zone defenses. Coaches who once frowned upon zones rely on them, while those who used zones all along have elevated their team's defenses to new levels of intensity and execution.

Examples abound. Everyone who follows the college game knows of the tenacious matchup zone played by Coach John Chaney's Temple University Owls. Year in and year out Temple is among the nation's stingiest teams in terms of points allowed and opponents' field-goal percentage. No change there! But how about the long-term change legendary former Princeton University Coach Pete Carill made from man-to-man to zone defensive philosophy? More recently, North Carolina's Dean Smith coached his 1994-95 team to the NCAA Final Four, in part by using more zone defense than any Tar Heel team in the last 20 years. Jim Boeheim took his Syracuse team to the 1996 NCAA championship game largely on the strength of a stifling 2-3 zone defense.

Even coaches with reputations for demanding tough, man-to-man defense, such as Duke University's Mike Krzyzewski, occasionally employ zone defenses. In today's college game the coach who relies exclusively on man-to-man defense is rare indeed. It's easy for me to put this into perspective. Every team we faced during the 1993-94 and '94-95 seasons—a total of 57 games —played at least some zone defense. Opponents included Wake Forest, Alabama, Illinois, Penn State, Providence, Nebraska and Alabama-Birmingham, to name a few. And yes, we mix in zone defenses as part of our overall scheme at the College of Charleston. We believe that the ability to change defenses contributes greatly to our success.

No single explanation exists for the zone phenomenon. The increased number of overpowering inside players, the proliferation of players with unstoppable one-on-one moves, the desire to minimize foul trouble, the belief that zone defense is easier to teach than man-to-man, and many other factors have contributed to the increased use of zones.

But none of that matters when the game is on the line and the opposition is playing zone defense. That's when you face the bottom line.

You might as well face it now. If you're going to develop a consistent winner at any level, from grade school to college, men or women, your team must be able to attack zone defenses.

I'm not talking about creating and taking nothing but perimeter jump shots. The jump shot is a useful weapon against the zone. But as every coach knows, if you live by the jump shot, you die by the jump shot. Do that and your team will never be as successful as it should be.

The alternative is a well-conceived, multifaceted system that combines elements of inside and outside offense to attack and defeat zone defenses where they thrive—in the half-court setting. I have adopted that system. Every coach should. That's what this book is all about. Zone defenses should be beaten. I want to help you get the job done.

Take the correct approach, and your offense can generate high percentage shots. You can free your top shooters and get the ball to your inside players where they can do the most damage. You can create three-on-two, two-on-one, and one-on-zero advantages on the offensive boards. Think of yourself as responding to the challenge of changing times, much as a corporation continually adapts and modernizes to satisfy a changing market.

The zone defense has come a long way. It wears clever disguises and sports constantly changing looks. It offers match-up potential and the ability to overplay your top shooter right out of business. It has become many modern coaches' defense of choice.

Meanwhile, offensive systems against the zone rely all too often on the age-old concept that the ball moves faster than defenders can react. Ball movement is great. But what about player movement? Combine ball movement, player movement, and a system of screens, and you can free up outside shooters, create opportunities for inside players, and turn your post player into a scorer and distributor.

Add it up and you can put the defense back where it belongs—on the defensive. But you need a system. I'll walk you through mine step-by-step, from basic principles to the final payoff. Together we'll pick apart the "feared" zone defense.

Actually, there's nothing to fear. The zone defense concedes a variety of benefits to a patient, well schooled offense. Unlike a tough, man-to-man defense, the zone allows an offense to get a shot when and where it wants one, with three bonuses: With sure passes, the offense commits fewer turnovers; shooters have more time to do their thing; and offensive rebounders can anticipate their teammates' shots and take advantage of the zone's inherent weaknesses in rebounding.

Consider another benefit. Too many people think playing a zone allows defenders to rest. To the contrary, a well-conceived, offensive game plan makes a zone defense sweat, while the attacking team's players have a moment or two to catch their breath.

There's another factor involved here. Many teams employ the zone as their primary defense, their bread and butter. By beating their zone defenses you may force them to

There's another factor involved here. Many teams employ the zone as their primary defense, their bread and butter. By beating their zone defenses you may force them to abandon their game plan. As a coach, you know that rarely works. You also know what does work.

The following chapters contain elements of what has worked for some legendary coaches: Clair Bee, Nat Holman, Joe Lapchick, and Lou Carnesecca. In my years as a player for Lapchick at St. John's University, as an assistant coach under Carnesecca at St. John's, and during my three-year stint with the New York Nets of the American Basketball Association, I was exposed to some of the game's great minds. I learned a lot of basketball watching fellow coaches frantically moving furniture around an office to simulate game situations. I did a great deal of learning at dining tables where salt and pepper shakers were put to offensive and defensive tasks and where many napkins were used to create now-famous diagrams. And then there was the actual game experience.

Zone defenses? In those days, the 1960s and 1970s, St. John's faced the Philadelphia schools on a regular basis. At that time St. Joe's, Villanova, Temple, and Penn played some of the best zone defense in the country. They were coached by excellent teachers and motivators like Jack Ramsay, Harry Litwack, and Jack Kraft. When you faced guys like those you either had a solid idea of what you were trying to do against zone defenses, or you lost.

Many of the basic principles in this book were generated in those days. I've supplemented them with ideas from a new generation of coaches and from strategies I've developed during 17 years as head coach at the College of Charleston.

Ideas are a big part of any successful program. I know all games are won or lost on the court, but every coach should be a little bit of a dreamer. I hope this book encourages you to think about the game—to daydream a little—and gives you the tools to turn some of those dreams into reality.

John Kresse
College of Charleston

CONTENTS

Page

Foreword 3
How This Book Will Help Your Program 4

SECTION I: PREPARING FOR SUCCESS

Chapter 1: Basic Principles: Rules to Win By 9
Chapter 2: The Balanced Machine 27
Chapter 3: Planning Each Trip Downcourt 35

SECTION II: CONTINUITIES AND SET PLAYS

Chapter 4: The Continuity Split 41
Chapter 5: The Continuity 13 47
Chapter 6: The Continuity BC 53
Chapter 7: The Continuity Blue 63
Chapter 8: The Continuity Special 69
Chapter 9: The Continuity Gold 75
Chapter 10: Set Plays: The Red Series 81
Chapter 11: Set Plays: Attacking From the Rear 97

SECTION III: SPECIAL SITUATIONS

Chapter 12: Three-Point Shots: Zone-Busters 101
Chapter 13: Inbounds Plays 115

About the Authors 126

CHAPTER 1

Basic Principles: Rules to Win By

Over the course of my career I have developed a list of basic principles for attacking zone defenses in the half-court setting. Some of these principles are strategic; others deal with technique; and still others are more philosophical in nature.

I don't think there's any mystery to the fact that the best way to attack a zone defense is by outrunning it—using a fast-breaking offense to beat the zone before it has a chance to set up. I'll leave it up to each coach to install his or her system for fast-breaking. In this book, I'll show you what to do when the fast break isn't there.

Here, then, are 11 basic principles for attacking zones in the half-court setting. Study these principles. They'll help you understand material in subsequent chapters and they'll give you and your players a foundation to build upon.

Recognizing the Zone

With the advent of changing defenses it is important to recognize whether you are facing a regular zone, a match-up zone, or a man-to-man. I liken this to a doctor studying a patient's symptoms in order to make an informed diagnosis. The doctor can't treat the patient before recognizing the illness. As a basketball team, you can't attack a defense until you recognize it.

Since regular zones (2-1-2, 2-3, 1-2-2, 3-2 and 1-3-1) assign defenders specific sections of the court rather than opposing players, you can recognize the defense by sending a cutter from the top of the key, wing, foul line, or corner to the basket and then to the other side of the floor. If your opponent is playing man-to-man defense a defender will stay with the cutter from one side of the floor to the other.

Zones are employed to take advantage of defensive players' individual skills, whether the skills are to steal the ball, to deny inside play, or to intimidate and to block shots. Zones are also employed to take away offensive players' strengths. This explains why you'll see a variety of zone defenses. Each does its job in a specific fashion, presumably the fashion best suited to the defensive personnel on the floor and least likely to concede attacking players the shots they want.

The 2-1-2 and 2-3 zones (Diagrams 1-1 and 1-2) are designed to minimize strong inside play by an opposing offense. These zones employ at least three big players who form a triangle around the basket as in a 2-1-2, or stand three-across from block to basket to other block. The 2-1-2 and 2-3 zones generally deploy their guards out front. The weakness of this type of zone is that it quite often concedes the top-of-the-key shot, the wing shot, or the down-the-middle shot.

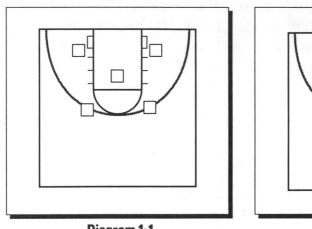

Diagram 1-1

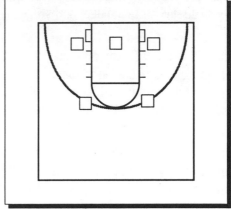

Diagram 1-2

Odd-man-front zones (1-2-2, 3-2, 1-3-1) employ a player on top of or in front of the zone, and then station the other four players differently.

The 1-2-2 and 3-2 zones are very similar. In the 1-2-2, (Diagram 1-3) the front player may extend himself to cover the top-of-the-key shot more. A 3-2 (Diagram 1-4) may be flatter across the top, deploying three defenders in a line across the front of the

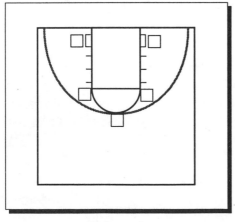

Diagram 1-3

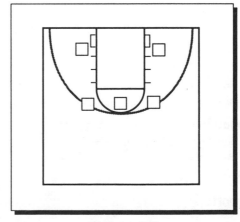

Diagram 1-4

zone. These two zones take away top-of-the-key and wing shots but they are vulnerable in the middle and sometimes in the corner.

The 1-3-1 zone (Diagram 1-5) covers the top of the key, the wings, the foul-line area, and the low-post area. However, it is vulnerable, especially in the corners and sometimes on top, should the wings drop too far.

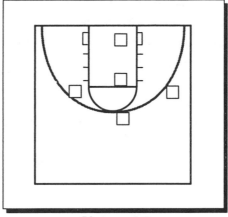

Diagram 1-5

A match-up zone employs five defensive players in the areas where the offense originates. If an offense shows a 1-3-1 attack, the defense immediately reacts and shows a 1-3-1 zone to match up with the five offensive players. If the offense shows a 2-1-2 set, the defense immediately reacts and deploys in what looks like a 2-1-2 zone.

The key in attacking a match-up is to use offensive players one-on-one with and without the ball. When a player cuts from one side of the court to the other, the defensive players must "pass off" the offensive player to a defender in another area of the court. After passing off a player the defender returns to his area of responsibility and seeks out an offensive player in that area. Areas are a little wider in a match-up zone and communication is the key to making it work.

If the offense becomes stagnant, it plays right into the hands of the match-up zone. Very few players will find open areas or gaps for shots. So to be successful against a match-up, you need cutting, flashing, and screening. This makes it difficult for the zone to adjust to both player and ball movement.

Since a match-up is so similar to man-to-man, you can create one-on-one opportunities facing the basket or you can create post-up situations for one-on-one play inside. You can treat a match-up somewhat like a man-to-man defense. You could actually run your man-to-man offense against a match-up defense. We don't because our zone offense offers so much movement and screening and picking that it is similar to some man-to-man offenses.

Another type of zone defense you see from time to time is the combination (box-and-one, diamond-and-one, triangle-and-two).

The traditional box-and-one (Diagram 1-6) deploys four players in a zone with two up front, usually at each elbow, and two players in the back on the blocks. The fifth defender plays a very tough denial-type defense on his man all over the court. Should his man receive a pass, the individual defender receives very strong support from his teammates.

The diamond-and-one (Diagram 1-7) is another form of the box and-one. Four defenders deploy in a zone with one player out front, one player on either side of the one-man front, and one taller player in the back of the diamond. Again, the defense stays with many one-on-one principles in playing the targeted offensive player with and without the ball.

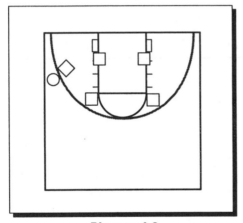

Diagram 1-6

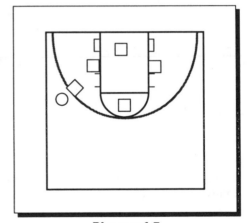

Diagram 1-7

The triangle-and-two (Diagrams 1-8 and 1-9) is geared to detain the two best offensive players or scorers. There are two forms of the triangle-and-two. Both play man-to-man defense on two players. One triangle has a one-man front with the other two players stationed behind the one player in the block areas. The other triangle features a defender in each elbow area with a taller player under the basket.

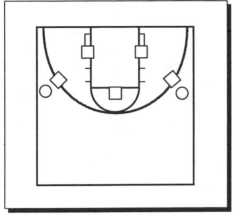

Diagram 1-8

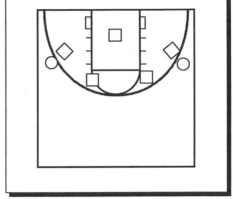

Diagram 1-9

Recognizing these zones is all-important in attacking them successfully. The box-and-one is recognizable because four defenders form a zone and one plays man-to-man. Again, the original premise of sending a cutter through can be applied to a box-and-one. If there is doubt and a player thinks he is being played one-on-one or man-to man he should be sent through as a cutter. To determine whether the other defenders are playing zone you can easily send another cutter through the defense and observe how he is guarded.

To recognize the triangle-and-two, send players who are being played man-to-man from one side of the court to the other. Check the other three defenders by sending a third player through.

Combinations are visible to the trained eye. The match-up is probably the toughest zone to recognize. It can look like man-to-man. Nowadays, teams are sending a defensive player almost from one side of the court to the other.

One way you may help yourself recognize and prepare for specific defenses is by scouting. If you have the manpower and time to scout future opponents you can gain a substantial edge. Rather than waiting for the game to begin and making a trip downcourt to determine an opposing defense you can recognize and prepare for some defenses in advance. Chances are, an opposing coach will use many of the same defenses from game to game because he has tailored his defensive game plan to his players' skills.

The Poise-Patience Payoff

In our continuity and set-play offenses we rely on good execution to exploit zone defenses for high-percentage shots. If a high-percentage shot is created by one or two passes, fine. However, there is no guarantee that any offense, no matter how well-executed, will quickly produce the kind of shot we want. If the offense doesn't click immediately, maturity and teamwork are keys. A mature, well-drilled team is prepared to make as many passes as are necessary to exploit zone defenses.

This is particularly important given some zones' tendency to "let up" after a certain amount of time or number of passes. I have found that some zone defenses don't sustain a high level of effort or intensity. After "X" number of passes individual defenders lack concentration and aggressiveness. Often, all it takes is patience to find a weak link: a player who doesn't fulfill his role or a weak area that suddenly appears.

Continuities are geared for one or two passes and a high-percentage shot. If that shot isn't available, ball reversal, player movement, and a few more passes are necessary to create a scoring opportunity.

Set plays put the primary scoring responsibility on one or two players who are either open or covered after the prescribed passes. Should the scorers be covered, the offense must have the patience to reset to another attack.

When there is no shot clock an offense can do whatever is necessary to create a high-percentage scoring opportunity. But remember, even with the 35-second shot clock employed at the college level, there is usually plenty of time to rethink and reset. Thirty-five seconds can be an eternity, especially when you're trying to sustain an intense defensive effort.

Timing: Finding and Hitting Openings

Suppose you have a 10 a.m. appointment to meet with a business associate. Get there at 9:30 and you waste 30 minutes waiting. Get there at 10:30 and chances are your associate is already gone.

Timing is just as important in basketball. With split-second timing you can find the open man or one who will be most effective with the right pass and catch.

In our offense we usually look for one or two options. Then we quickly look to the weak side, where we can catch the zone napping or outnumber defenders in a different area of the court. Ball and player movement to the weak side before defenders have time to react often catches the zone. A cut from one side of the court to the other or a flash of the ball should be quick and hard, but it should also be under control. If a pass receiver is out of control, he is not an effective threat to score or pass.

Players should establish a specific space-time relationship between themselves and the ball. Proper spacing and timing create problems for a zone that is intended to match up, clog passing lanes, and deny the ball inside.

Players should end up 12 to 15 feet apart so that no single defender can guard two offensive players by himself. Whether you are facing the basket or have your back to it, this spatial relationship is most important. Having two outlet passes is good. Having three is even better, especially if they are in proper position for the sure, snappy pass.

One pass that involves something other than traditional 12-to-15 foot spacing is the skip pass to the weak side. This effective pass should always be an option, especially if the zone concentrates on the strong side or where the ball is. We'll talk more about the skip pass later.

For now, it's most important to understand that repetition is the key to developing the kind of timing you need to attack and defeat zone defenses. By dummy and live work in practice, passes, cuts, screens, and gap, step-ins become second nature. And that's critical. Once on the court players can't afford to think about timing. It must be automatic.

Passing

For virtually every score, except a rebound and stickback, a player makes a correct pass as the opportunity presents itself. A correct pass is even more important in attacking zone defenses. Zones take away a lot of one-on-one play and dribbling. They can, however, be particularly vulnerable to crisp, well-chosen passes.

On the perimeter, I prefer the two-hand chest pass. It's quick, efficient, and easy to teach. Also, the two-hand chest pass travels faster than the bounce or alley-oop pass, and ball reversal demands moving the ball from one player to the next with the utmost speed.

The bounce pass can be effective when feeding the low or mid post. When installing and teaching zone defenses coaches often demand that players keep their hands up. Meanwhile, a player receiving a bounce pass usually has his knees bent and can easily turn or spin either way for a strong move to the basket. Defenders guarding players with their backs to the basket have a hard time stealing the bounce pass. Usually, taller players in this defensive position have a difficult time reaching around and down; consequently, they commit fouls.

The bounce pass can also be effective on the backdoor play which often is available against zones, especially match-ups. Such situations as a forward backdoor with a guard pass, a forward backdoor with a high-post pass, or a high-post cut with a low-post pass employ the bounce pass effectively.

The alley-oop pass can be very effective in zone offense. In fact, three of our set plays employ the alley-oop pass to a leaper attacking from the rear of the defense.

Quite often you can sneak a player to the weakside block or attack the zone from behind and throw over the defenders. Weakside defenders often have problems with match-up responsibilities. The airborne attacking player has the huge advantage of knowing precisely when and where the ball should be thrown.

When zones pressure the ball or really sag to prevent interior passing, the skip or crosscourt pass becomes a potent weapon. A good skip pass can lead to either a jump shot or a strong penetration move. The defense often rushes out of control to cover the unattended shooter who can then drive right by for an easier shot or pass.

Screening the back of the zone can create openings for effective use of the crosscourt or skip pass. Since weakside defenders are almost always stationed in the lane, a spot-up shooter can receive a skip pass and take an open jump shot or pass to a screener posting up before the defense has time to react.

You needn't always pass the ball to make effective use of passing. Why?

Although a zone defense is supposed to shift only with an actual pass, some zones and defenders anticipate ball movement and leave players and areas open on a legitimate ball fake. A perimeter defender often anticipates being two or three passes from the ball. A good ball fake can catch that defender by surprise and lead to a high-percentage scoring opportunity.

Ball fakes aren't effective only on the perimeter. The low, mid, or high post can open up on a ball fake, as a defender in the lane may prematurely rush to another defensive responsibility, thereby leaving an attacking player unattended.

Quite often, the player who just passed can immediately receive the ball back after a good ball fake. If the zone anticipates ball reversal the original passer is often open for a jump shot or penetration move.

Remember, since all five players in a zone defense are coached to move and shift with each pass, a good ball fake often catches one or two defenders out of position.

The Pass Receiver as Triple Threat
Now that we've briefly discussed passing and its role in our zone offenses, let's consider the role of the pass receiver as triple threat.

Whether an attacking player faces toward the basket or away from it, he must be able to shoot, pass, or drive upon receiving the ball. The triple-threat position makes each offensive player a potentially dangerous weapon in our zone-attack arsenal. The good offensive player thinks "score" whenever he receives a pass. But if the zone reacts correctly and takes away the high-percentage shot or drive, the offensive player must be prepared to make a good pass.

Our zone offenses, whether continuities or set plays, give attacking players the options they need to be truly effective triple-threat weapons.

In our system a high-percentage shot from the outside is defined simply as an unforced shot within a player's range. Some players have the arm and leg strength to shoot over defenders. In our offensive system, however, most shooters facing the basket have the luxury of distance from the defense and time to set up.

A high-percentage inside shot can also be uncontested. But more often than not, it will require the shooter to make a strong or elusive move or shoot over a defender.

Since we don't want to dribble or drive too often against a zone defense, the next best option, if no shot is available, is a well-conceived pass to another player. A player receiving a pass should be aware of his various options. In short, which players are open and where are they?

Some passing options create triangles, outnumber the defense, or rely on a skip pass to an open player.

You should not, however, forget the dribble-drive. This attractive option develops when an attacking player in triple-threat position suddenly sees a lane to the basket or is covered by an out-of-position defender. In our zone offenses we often create situations in which defenders are forced to rush the ball. The dribble-drive exploits such defenders.

Dribbling

Despite the universally accepted conclusion that passing is more important than dribbling in zone offense, the dribble is a useful tool in attacking zones.

The dribble is very effective in initiating a set, half-court offense. By initially taking the dribble away from your intended area of attack you accomplish two things. First, the dribble effectively creates a passing lane to your intended receiver. If you initially bring the ball to the area you intend to attack, you may see overplay or denial defense. However, by quickly changing direction and taking the ball opposite to the weak side you can catch the defense before it reacts for the overplay. Combine the same dribbling device with quick player movement from one side of the court to the other and you'll receive a second benefit: two-on-one, three-on-two, and four-on-three overload situations.

Once you're into your zone attack you'll see openings for the dribble-drive. We use the dribble-drive most often from the wing areas and from the short corners. From the key area there are simply too many defenders to beat consistently with the dribble-drive. We also don't advocate driving from the post. That position is best used for a shot or a quick pass for a sure shot, as the post player can see the whole court for a variety of effective passes.

But from the areas 15 to 17 feet from the basket on either side, attacking players are in optimum position for one-on-one opportunities on quick ball reversal. If the lane is there take it. If not, a good one-on-one player may be able to create a lane. It is important that the driving player, no matter how capable, be careful not to charge. Zone defenders often step in at the end of a drive, hoping to draw a charge. Remind your players of this possibility and drill them on pulling up for jump shots in practice. See the lane and attack it, but don't play into the defense's hands by driving out of control.

A player with his back to the basket must also be selective in using the dribble. Perimeter or blind-side defenders often use the element of surprise to steal the ball in this situation. While I don't advocate overuse of the dribble in this situation, I've learned never to say never. A good strong move using the dribble can be very effective, but players should be aware of the possibility of having the ball stolen.

The dribble can also be used to exploit gaps. Indiana coach Bob Knight does an excellent job of getting his players to explode past defenders. If you can beat two-fifths or three-fifths of the defense with the dribble and then pull up for a shot or pass, you're making positive things happen.

With a hard but controlled dribble into a gap you often force two defenders to play the ball. You split the defense and make it impossible to match up effectively. Just remember, when dribbling into the gap, do so with the shot or the next pass in mind.

Shooting

In most zone offenses—and our continuities and set plays are no exception—players know where and when they will have opportunities to shoot. With players continually running routes and patterns to create shots in certain areas, spot-up shooting drills in practice are an absolute must.

Let's take a look at areas of the court where the best, highest percentage shots occur. In later chapters you'll learn how to create these shots.

The perimeter is a good place to start. Because many zone defenses are designed to choke off inside offense, the jump shot is an ever-present option. The trick is producing high-percentage jump shots— good shots taken by good shooters.

On the perimeter, the top-of-the-key or down-the-middle shot is a good bet. More often than not a good shooting guard will connect from straight on.

The foul-line-extended area, three or four feet beyond the elbow, is another high-percentage area for guards. It offers the additional benefit of excellent lanes for passes into the paint.

Shooting guards and forwards can make good use of the wing areas, which offer the triple option of shooting, passing the ball into the posts, or passing it back to the top of the key. Against certain 2-3 and 2-1-2 zones, the wings are often gap areas. Encourage your shooters to step in for the high-percentage jumper.

The corners, located 18 to 20 feet from the basket, are familiar ground for forwards and can also be utilized by shooting guards. A good shooting guard moves to the corners for jump shots or occasional dump-in passes to the low- or mid-post. The short corners are located closer to the baseline, about 15 feet from the basket.

The jump shot is still available, but an even more attractive option involves a quick dribble to the baseline behind the zone for a lay-up. Facing the basket, the short-corner player has excellent angles for passes to the low- and mid-posts. Without the ball the short corner player is a continual threat to sneak behind the zone for an alley-oop pass.

Dribble past one or two defenders and you're in an area we call the gut. The gut is the perfect spot for a quick pull-up move, capped off with a jump shot or pass. The gut areas aren't for everyone. We prefer to limit dribbling when attacking zones. But we also recognize and utilize physical talent. If you have a player who combines the ball-handling skills, explosiveness, and leaping ability to penetrate the gut effectively, don't discourage him.

The high post is an attractive area for a player who combines effective jump shooting with court vision and passing skills. A good jump shooter not only finds uncontested shots; he often is covered by a shorter defender he can simply shoot over. As a passer, a player in the high post has options left and right to the elbows, wings, and corners, with back-door possibilities on either block.

The mid-post is often accessible from out top, the elbows, the wings, and the corners. From the mid-post, your best options are a turn-around jump shot, a jump hook, or a pure hook.

The low-post is a power position. Passes from the high-post, wings, and corners create the 12-to-15-foot look and entry. While we generally discourage dribbling in the low-post, it's another one of those "never say never" situations. With or without a dribble, the player should use the same shots as produced in the mid-post, with lay-ups thrown in for good measure.

One additional bonus: Establish your big people, get the ball to the mid-post and low-post often enough, and defenders often react by swarming or diving in. Should that occur, a quick pass back outside usually finds a spot-up jump shooter for an uncontested shot.

Offensive Rebounding: The Edge
Offensive rebounding is a high priority in our zone attack—and for good reason. Many zone defenses, no matter how well schooled in the checking-out department, concede openings to well-positioned offensive rebounders.

In many instances zone defenders are thinking "area" rather than "man," so they lose sight of an offensive rebounder making a move to the basket. In certain instances two potential offensive rebounders are in one defender's area. At times, weakside defenders pack in too tightly under the basket and can't possibly box out on long rebounds.

If your team plays zone defense you know these problems all too well.

In our set plays, designed to create a specific scoring threat, our offensive rebounders have the tremendous advantage of knowing where and when shots will occur. Therefore, our offensive rebounders can anticipate shots and can maneuver inside rear defenders for optimum rebounding position.

In our continuities we are looking for certain options that inevitably produce most of the shots. Once again, the same edge in anticipation is available. Because continuities are designed to "continue" from one side of the court to the other, it is vital that prospective offensive rebounders retain their concentration, stay in their patterns, and be prepared to regain a positional edge on ball reversal.

The logic here is obvious. By designing situations that involve high-percentage passing, dribbling, and scoring opportunities, you'll inevitably improve your offensive rebounding. Don't get the wrong idea. Nothing is automatic. Offensive rebounding still takes a lot of hard, physical work. But by knowing where all the players are located in set plays and continuities, you can manufacture three-on-two, two on-one, and one-on-zero offensive rebounding advantages. And it's tough to beat a one-on-zero advantage isn't it?

It takes careful study by a coach to take full advantage of these opportunities. Look at the position of all five offensive and all five defensive players on the blackboard and on the court. Examine when and where shots will be taken. You'll find yourself forming triangles (players on each block and one in front of the basket) and gaining pivotal numerical advantages.

This is "the edge."

The Seven Triangles: Creating Overloads
You're all familiar with the shape of a triangle—a three-sided figure with three points.

On a basketball court triangles are formed by three players, 12 to 15 feet from each other, and each a threat to score. Usually triangles are formed by quick player movement and our zone attack is no exception. Our players don't remain in any one position for more than one or two passes.

In the ideal situation the triangle is an overload—three offensive players guarded by two defenders. Should that occur, we look for any of the three players to score or to make the proper pass for a high-percentage scoring opportunity.

Should the zone shift quickly to counter the overload, offensive players can still establish excellent one-on-one position, either facing or with their backs to the basket.

Any three players, regardless of position, can form effective triangles. The important thing is that players fill holes in the defense when forming triangles.

Diagrams 1-10 through 1-16 show the seven triangles that occur naturally within our zone attack. Familiarize yourself with them and you'll recognize them more easily in later chapters when we diagram continuities and set plays.

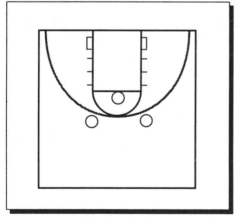

Diagram 1-10

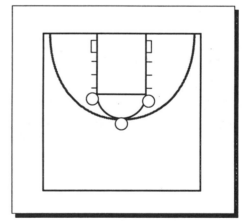

Diagram 1-11

Diagram 1-12

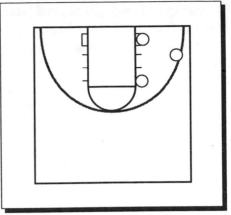

Diagram 1-13

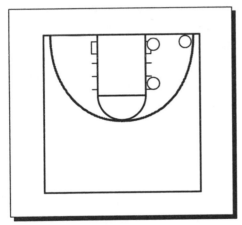

Diagram 1-14

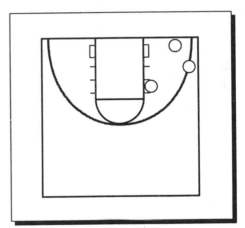

Diagram 1-15

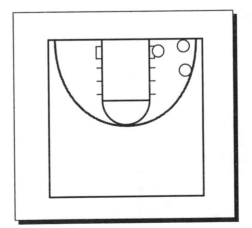

Diagram 1-16

Screening the Front, Back, and Interior of Zones

In years gone by, the accepted method of attacking zone defenses placed emphasis on ball movement. Stationary players whipped the ball around the zone as if it were a hot potato.

To a point, I agree with this philosophy. Quick ball movement is one element of zone offense. But let's not stop there. Let's incorporate certain elements of man-to-man offense, such as player movement and effective screening. Think of it this way: no defender enjoys fighting through the kind of well-set screens he encounters in man-to-man defense. So why not incorporate screens in zone offense? They can be just as effective.

Our screens are set by our forward or center and are as big and wide as possible. We set screens early to assure they are stationary and not illegal. After all, who needs a dumb foul and turnover? Timing and control are the key factors in avoiding illegal screens. By quickly establishing which player must be screened, then moving no more than ten feet to set the screen, we develop the desired control.

Interior screens are set by forwards and centers for each other. We usually screen the inside or back defenders. Players using these screens must be ready to cut or flash to the ball. Our cutters usually run directly off the screener's hip or shoulder to the low-, mid-, or high-post.

There is a substantial difference between an interior screen (Diagram 1-17) and a screen against the back of a zone (Diagram 1-18). Interior screens are set for players coming into the lane. Back screens also screen big players, but usually are set for a corner jump shot. With an effective screen against the back of a zone, shooting guards and forwards often find themselves in ideal, unguarded position for a jump shot or dump-in pass.

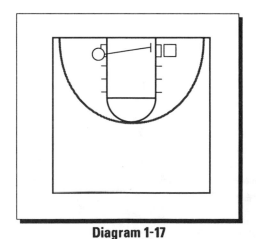

Diagram 1-17

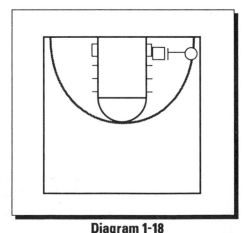

Diagram 1-18

Screens against defenders on the top or front of a zone (Diagram 1-19) create jump-shot and pick-and-roll openings for guards or small forwards. We use a dribble block in our set-play formation to gain this particular advantage.

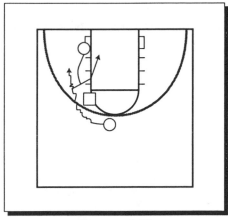

Diagram 1-19

Attacking From the Rear: What They Don't See Can Hurt Them
Is there any more spectacular offensive play than the alley-oop pass and slam-dunk? It's more than just two points. It's an instant lift for the offense and a real demoralizer for the defense.

It's also a prime example of attacking from the rear of the defense—something we like to do in our zone attacks.

Cutting and moving without the ball is an essential ingredient in our zone offense. In zone alignments defenders are required to cover surprisingly large areas of the court. Why make it any easier for them by standing around on offense? Move and cut before the defense can react and chances are you'll have a jump shot, post play, or passing lanes.

We have found that one of the better ways to exploit these openings is by routing players "behind" the zone where they can't be seen.

Guards attack from the rear to the wings and corners for jump shots and dump-in passes. Shooting forwards can take the same routes for outside shots. Frontline players, whose forte is power, can attack from the rear into a variety of areas—the low-, mid-, and high-posts, the lane, and of course, straight to the hoop for an alley-oop pass.

In subsequent chapters we'll demonstrate this type of movement with and without screens.

CHAPTER 2

The Balanced Machine

Balance. Talk to a coach of any team sport and chances are, sooner or later, the conversation will touch on the concept of balance. A football coach wants offense and defense. Within his offense he wants running and passing. Within his running game, he wants a guy who can pound inside for tough yards teamed with a speedster who can run outside. And ideally, both backs can catch passes and block.

Balance within balance within balance within balance. Give me that kind of balance, the coach will tell you, and he'll win the Super Bowl. Basketball offers similar rewards for balance.

To my way of thinking, the perfect basketball team would feature five all-around players, all of whom could shoot out the lights, dribble circles around defenders, make the perfect pass to the open man, rebound like demons, run the floor, and, of course, play defense. Wouldn't it be nice to coach that kind of team?

Unfortunately, there are only so many Michael Jordans, Magic Johnsons, Larry Birds, and Oscar Robertsons. You're blessed if you have one of them, much less five.

Because there are so few "complete" players, coaches must continually evaluate players and make tough choices.

Joe Lapchick, a member of the original Celtics and my coach at St. John's University, had his own system of evaluating players. When evaluating guards, Coach Lapchick considered three areas: scoring, ballhandling, and defense. If a guard could do one of those three things well, he'd struggle for playing time; with two skills, he'd play a lot; with three, he'd be outstanding.

When evaluating forwards and centers the criteria were scoring, rebounding, and defense. Again, two skills made for an effective player while three foreshadowed stardom.

In my years as a high school, NAIA, NCAA, and pro coach, I've tried Coach Lapchick's system, and it works.

How does this affect the "balanced machine"? To be a consistent winner at any level you must have the necessary components both offensively and defensively. Since this book deals primarily with offensive play, I won't dwell on defensive skills, other than to say that every team needs two or three really good defenders to win. Stoppers in the backcourt and up front are necessities. Keep this in mind when evaluating players' offensive skills and contributions. All offensive skills being equal, go with the defensive stopper. Depending on the situation, give thought to going with a skilled defender even if his offensive skills don't quite match another player's weapons.

Position by Position

Here's what we look for from each position on the court.

In our half-court offense, the point guard combines elements of court savvy, communication, ballhandling, shooting, and defense. Before anything else, the point guard, in conjunction with the coach, must recognize the type of defense the opponent is playing, then verbally or by hand signal communicate the continuity or set play we want to run. Once that's done, the point guard initiates the offense off the pass or dribble and sets our offense in motion. The point guard should be a good passer, with some ability to penetrate and create scoring opportunities in the right situation.

With all of these responsibilities, the point guard isn't a primary scoring threat. But this player's willingness to step in and hit the occasional jump shot goes a long way toward keeping zone defenses honest.

The point guard should think defense while on offense. Should a shot be missed or an errant pass be thrown, someone must protect the backcourt. From a position on the perimeter the point guard is a logical candidate for that duty.

The point guard's backcourt partner, often referred to as the shooting guard, should live up to that name. Unless challenged by a good shooter or two, most zone defenses will sag or collapse to deny a team's inside offense. The shooting guard, also occasionally called the off guard, should make zones pay for sagging inside. He should be able to spot-shoot from those areas where our continuities and set plays create shots.

Recognizing the shooting guard's skills, many zones will overplay him in certain high-percentage areas, so the shooting guard's ability to move without the ball is critical. We help our shooting guard get open with screens and picks. It's up to the shooting guard to take advantage of a good pick with a smart cut to an open area.

If the zone rushes out to cover the shooting guard or if the shooting guard sees gaps in the defense, the drive, pull-up jump shot, or penetration and pass may be available.

We have other considerations: rebounding and defense. We like to send our shooting guard to the offensive boards, especially if our opponent doesn't employ a fast-paced, transition-minded offense. Should our opponent try to run, the shooting guard must have the quickness and presence of mind to sprint back and cover the backcourt.

So there's the ideal backcourt. Two players combine to give effective court generalship, ballhandling, perimeter offense, and defense—in a word, balance.

Balance is also important at the two forward positions. One of the forwards, usually the smaller of the two, should be competent from the perimeter as a shooter and passer. Like the shooting guard, he should be an accomplished spot shooter, usually from the wing or corner areas. Also, the small forward should be able to move effectively without the ball and possess an effective one-on-one game.

Moving to the outside and inside is an effective weapon for the ideal small forward. Flashing into the lane to the low-, mid-, and high-post areas will lead to post-up situations and turnaround jump shots.

We always go to the offensive boards with three big players. The small forward should get his share of offensive rebounds due to quickness and maneuverability, combined with the anticipation factor inherent in our continuities and set plays.

While the small forward assumes perimeter responsibilities, the other forward's strength should be just that—strength. Sure, it's great if your power forward doubles as an outside threat, but that's not a necessity. An occasional 15-footer from the short corner, combined with baseline driving ability will suffice.

Inside, the power forward must have post-up and offensive rebounding skills. He must be able to flash and move to create those two openings. The power forward sets screens for guards, the other forward, and the center. The power forward uses screens too.

In summary, the power forward is the blue-collar worker on your team, performing a lot of tough, thankless jobs. If the small forward provides flash, the power forward provides crash. Again, balance.

Having discussed guards and forwards, that leaves the center. A complete center is tough to find. In our offense, the center is a focal point in many continuities and set plays. He is the hub of our wheel, making things happen all around.

By pointing the ball or flashing into the lane area, the center is a direct threat to pass to any of the other four players for an immediate score. So passing skills, particularly from the post areas, are important. Pass-catching skills are similarly important, whether as a release point against pressure or as a scoring threat.

As a scorer, the center relies on back-to-the-basket moves. Offensive rebounding is a must. We also use the center as a screener.

The center's offensive skills are important but they may be outweighed by defensive factors. The true shot-blocking center is a rare and valuable commodity. If you have one on your team don't talk yourself out of using him because he has certain offensive shortcomings. With hard work you can create and develop an adequate offensive player. You cannot create a great shot blocker.

Evaluation and Testing
I've told you what we look for. Now how do we find it?

How do we know which players will be most effective against zone defenses? Which guard has the unique package of skills required to run the show? Which guard and forward have the perimeter skills needed to keep zones honest? Who has the strength and persistence to play power forward? Do we have a true center? If not, who can fill that role?

Obviously, accurate evaluation and testing of players' skills make attacking zone defenses a much simpler task. Some players are simply better suited to attacking zone defenses. They have the combination of maturity and physical skill needed to bust zones. But how do you uncover those skills?

First, always assume you must start from scratch. By dummying (drilling without defense), we work on fundamentals and maneuvers in one-on-zero, two-on-zero, and three-on-zero situations. Tell and teach what has to be done then show players how to do it. Make sure your players do what you ask. All good coaches insist on execution at all levels, beginning with practice.

After dummying work against live defense. First, see how your players fare in one-on-one situations. Then expand your scope to the overall team picture. Look for examples of two-man and three-man basketball. Do your players see the game? Can they read defenses? Are they physical enough to win tough battles with the game on the line? Do they execute?

In tryouts, put your players through these basic situations giving them every benefit of the doubt. Take and give as much time as you can afford. If you start and finish with a single scrimmage you may overlook a player whose raw talent didn't shine through in a particular setting. Don't expect to see a bunch of complete players and don't judge solely by a player's bottom-line productivity in a single game. As a coach, a big part of your job is discovering players' innate abilities then developing and combining those skills into an effective unit.

Certain tools are particularly handy when attacking zone defenses. In recruiting or tryouts you should look for a zone-buster—a player with a fine eye and a good shot from the perimeter. Since our zone offenses readily create perimeter shots, and many zones concede them, having a specialist or two on hand for zone-busting duties can be the difference between victory and defeat.

The Value of True Depth
Throughout this chapter I have used the word "balance" repeatedly, often in the phrase "the balanced machine."

As everyone knows, no machine can function without spare parts. In fact, in some cases it's difficult to distinguish which parts are the spares and which are the originals.

Think of your car. During the summer it rolls on standard-tread tires. During the winter, when faced with different road conditions, you may replace the regular tires with snow tires. Same machine. Different parts. Same result. You get where you're going.

Basketball teams also face changing conditions from game to game, occasionally from minute to minute. So why not change parts to achieve maximum performance?

This is where your bench comes into play. Ideally, you'll have a minimum of eight effective players, if only to give starters an occasional breather or to fill in in the event of player injury. If for that purpose alone, you should develop three effective guards, three forwards, and two centers. This is one kind of depth.

The other kind, true depth, is more valuable. True depth goes beyond giving a starter a breather. True depth gives a coach the flexibility to adapt to changing conditions.

Let's say the other team plays man-to-man defense. Early in the game your players establish a substantial edge in individual match-ups. Sensing this, the opposing coach switches to a zone defense, negating some of your one-on-one and power advantages, while conceding perimeter jump shots.

Wouldn't it be nice to have an effective jump shooter, a true zone-buster, on the bench, just waiting for such an opportunity?

Maybe the zone-buster isn't a complete player. Maybe you don't want him or her on the floor 95 percent of the time. But a zone-buster certainly comes in handy when you need a couple of jumpers to loosen up a zone.

The point is to think of your bench as part of the truly balanced machine. Sure, you won't win with eight one-dimensional role-players. But then again, you probably won't win consistently without a few effective role-players—perhaps a zone-buster or a defensive stopper.

In developing depth, think of your players position by position. If you could, you'd have four guards, two point guards and two shooting guards. More likely, you'll have three guards. If that's the case, one of them must be able to play both positions.

Up front, you'd like four forwards and two centers, two players for each of three positions. As a minimum, you'll need three players capable of playing forward and two capable of playing center. For example, your starting power forward could be your backup center. You may find yourself substituting a small, zone-busting forward for a center, with your other forwards sliding over to other positions.

It's a bit of a chess game. The more pieces you have, the more likely you'll win. The player who can fill two positions effectively makes your job easier.

One thing is certain. To attack zone defenses with great success you'll need a unit that combines the type of patience, ballhandling, screening, and jump-shooting skills outlined previously in "Position by Position."

Be aware that some of those skills may be sitting on your bench just waiting to be turned loose against a zone.

CHAPTER 3

Planning Each Trip Downcourt

You've evaluated your personnel. You've discovered, as I suggested in the previous chapter, that certain players are better suited to attacking man-to-man defenses, while others have what it takes to dissect zones.

In short, you know what weapons are at your command. Now it's time to think about the other guy. What is your opponent trying to accomplish defensively and just how good a job is your opponent doing?

Things the Coach Must Know

In attacking zone defenses you need to know more than just what type of zone you're up against. You need to know the zone's tendencies—its strengths and weaknesses.

Some zones start tough and stay tough. Others don't sustain a high level of intensity and execution for more than five or six passes. Some zones play the perimeter wide and with a great deal of pressure, possibly conceding inside openings. Others sag to prevent inside passing but entertain the perimeter jump shot. Some zones can be screened effectively; others can't.

Know your opponent's tendencies as well as your own and you gain a tremendous advantage. Aside from scouting, the best way to reveal an opponent's strengths and weaknesses is by running a variety of continuities and set plays early in the game. You and your staff should observe the result of each trip down the floor, then verify your observations with the help of statistics and charts.

Are you banging the ball inside effectively? Stats and shot charts should tell you. Are you clicking at a high percentage from the perimeter? Again, stats and charts answer your question.

Spend the early part of a game gathering information, then put that information to good use at crunch time. Check your ammunition and your top guns won't jam when they have to get off a game-winning shot.

Continuities and Set Plays: Making the Right Decisions

I employ two basic approaches to attacking zone defense in a half-court setting. They are the continuity and the set play.

Let's start with the continuity. We employ six of them, each with well-defined strengths and benefits.

But first, what is a continuity? As its name implies, a continuity involves continual, patterned ball and player movement from one side of the court to the other. In theory, a continuity can run as long as necessary to create a high-percentage scoring opportunity. That may take one pass, seven or eight passes, or however many passes time allows and you prefer.

The continuity offers three distinct advantages. It places all players in a position to score, with particular emphasis on the inside game. It uses some screens against a zone's interior, a fairly new ploy that some teams may not be able to handle. And it can be employed as a time-killing device in late-game situations.

In the previous chapter on basic principles against all zone defenses I discussed the concept of triangles—three-man overloads in specific areas of a zone defense. Five of the seven basic triangles consist of either two post players and a perimeter player or a post player, a player in the short corner, and a perimeter player. The triangle is the basic building block of inside offense against zone defense. Continuities create triangles more often than set plays. That's why continuities are such an effective method of generating inside offense.

What does inside offense mean to your team? The immediate payoffs are obvious. You're working the ball inside for high-percentage shots. In the process, you may put opposing big men in foul trouble. But there's much more at stake.

If you create enough inside action, your opponent will probably move to cut off passing lanes to the posts and middle. Your opponent will go to the classic sagging zone. That's when opportunity jump shots will become available. If you produce an effective inside game and the defense "sells out" to stop the inside action, you will get the step-in jump shot or the skip pass for an open shot. This is what I mean when I say that continuities are inside-oriented with outside options. An uncontested jump shot is an excellent outside option.

By forcing an opponent to play a sagging zone defense, you also reduce your opponent's ability to sting you with the fast break. Players can't fly out of a sagging zone and guards usually find it difficult to set up in designated outlet areas—no runners, no outlets, no fast break.

One other benefit: You keep your big players happy. I know it's an old cliche, but it's also a fact. Give big players a piece of the action on offense, get them involved, and chances are they'll play a better game at the other end, where you really need them. A happy big player rebounds better, plays better defense, and is a better shot-blocker. What more can you want?

Unlike the continuity, which creates opportunities for all players, the set play is geared to go to one or two players. The set play goes by the logic that a team should create specific opportunities for its most gifted scorers.

Just as the scorer fills a role, other players have roles to fill. You need a good passer and a good screener to make set plays work. The role-players must understand the importance of what they're doing in a team setting. They must know their abilities and their teammates' abilities. As a coach, you must make certain statistics available to your players. Properly employed stats tell players not only what they have done, but what they are best capable of doing.

A rebounder collects rebounds. A passer racks up assists. A scorer scores points. When it's time for a basket, it's vital that the scorer has the ball in his hands when and where he needs it.

Once players recognize and accept their roles, the set play is a truly effective method of attacking zone defenses. You pinpoint the zone's weakness, whether it's an area or a specific defender, and you attack that weakness. A well-run set play is not unlike a surgical procedure. It's swift, clean, and precise, and good results will show-up on the scoreboard.

Most set plays offer a legitimate alternative to continuities. The continuity is inside-oriented with outside options. The set play is geared toward creating outside action.

Whether you emphasize inside or perimeter offense, a certain minimum balance is necessary to achieve overall success against zone defenses. In my 32 years as a coach I have never seen a team win with only inside power or outside shooting. Teams that attack zones successfully generally get the job done with a blend of five components: fast breaks, outside shooting, inside power, drives to the hoop, and follow-up baskets. We're primarily concerned with the half-court game so let's forget about the fast break for now. That leaves us with our half-court options—continuities and set plays.

Which strategy do you choose? Knowing your team's strengths and weaknesses, and having observed your opponent's tendencies, you can make an informed strategic decision.

As you will see in later chapters, continuities get more players actively involved in attacking the defense and possibly scoring. If the zone chooses to concentrate on your top scorers a continuity will lead to high-percentage scoring opportunities for your other players. With quick ball reversal you can attack either side of the zone. Also, by getting the ball inside you set up the quick, high-percentage pass back outside to spot-up shooters. This inside-out action can be a very effective weapon, as it defeats the zone's original intent of overplaying or outnumbering your top guns.

Certainly, if you can get the ball inside to players who either finish strong or pass back outside effectively, you put zone defenders in the uncomfortable position of having to make a decision. Do I stick with the top scorer or do I sag inside to help out? Quite often, a defender gets caught in between where he's of little or no value defensively.

If your team is geared to go to one or two primary scorers you may want to use our set-play offense. Most of our set plays are designed to create perimeter shots, although some are more inside oriented. If the defense reacts well to the immediate, primary offensive threat, inside opportunities will be available on a quick pass or on a fake pass.

Part of the beauty of our set-play offense is that all the plays originate from a 1-3-1 set. This makes it especially difficult for the defense to read or anticipate a given play.

One final note here. I think it's important to run a series of continuities in a row or a few set plays in succession. If one particular continuity is going well, you have the luxury of sticking with it or of mixing it with other continuities to give defenders a tougher time adjusting. Also consider which side of the defense you are attacking, whether to explore the zone or to exploit a specific defensive weakness. When running a series of set plays, take into consideration which of your players has the hot hand and see to it that he gets the ball often enough to rack up game-winning numbers.

Organization of Players
After trying to score from our fast-break or press attack we try to make the smoothest transition possible into our half-court zone attack.

Since our point guard initiates both our set-play and continuity offenses, we get the ball into his hands as quickly as possible. As explained previously, the point guard bridges the communication gap between coach and players.

How and when do we communicate?

At times, we run a series of up to four different continuities or set plays called before the game or during a timeout. In that instance, we don't verbally call or physically signal the plays we are running.

I know what you're thinking. Can I count on my players to handle that kind of mental load in pressure situations? I've found that with repetition and hard work in practices and scrimmages, players can handle this load. It's all part of attacking zone defenses. Think of it this way: The ability to remember and execute four plays is every bit as important in attacking zone defenses as are certain physical skills.

At other times, we call our next offensive play as early as possible, often when retreating on defense. If not then, you can call a play when taking the ball out after an opponent's field goal or when an opponent is shooting a foul shot.

On missed field goals—and we hope there are plenty of those—we call or signal our play as we bring the ball up in the backcourt. This early organization allows players a chance to think about and to plan the trip downcourt.

Once our players know the call and are in proper position to start the play the point guard initiates the play off the pass or dribble.

Just what is "proper position"?

We start our offense as close to the basket as possible so the initial pass receiver is in position for a high-percentage shot or pass. Given that strategy, it's obvious that all our continuities and set plays are most effective with a shooting guard who can bury the jumper off the first pass or who can make the proper pass for an even better scoring opportunity elsewhere.

Except for the continuities we call "Blue" and "13," it doesn't matter whether we play with a shooting forward or a power forward. The two positions are effectively interchangeable. In Blue and 13, you need one player who is more effective facing the basket for a shot, pass, or drive, and another who is stronger with his back to the basket or from the short corner.

Of course, surprises always occur and your team must be prepared to meet the challenge of sudden adjustments by the defense. Teams are changing defenses more than ever, double-teaming or trying to force the ball to one side of the court or the other.

How do you combat those changes? Obviously, recognition and immediate communication and adjustment are keys. One continuity doesn't work against all defenses. Then again, one defense doesn't work against all set plays or continuities. Players and coaches must see the defense and react accordingly.

Realizing that double-teams can occur at any time with little or no warning, we have built into our zone attack the ability to pass before the double-team is set. Two or three outlets are immediately available. Once the outlet is made, we have three options: the quick score, the pass for a score, or simply resuming our planned attack. For example, having an outlet at the high-post or top of the key, creating ball reversal, can get us a high-percentage shot from the weak side.

Should a team try to channel our offense to one side of the court we have similarly attractive options. We can try to change direction off the dribble, especially if we want to initiate our attack on the other side of the floor, or we can outlet the ball to another player, either a guard or a forward, who may break to the other side of the floor or who is stationed at the high-post.

If we want the point guard to initiate the offense off a pass or dribble to a certain player, the guard follows his pass, gets the ball back, and starts over.

CHAPTER 4

The Continuity Split

As its name implies, this offense finds the gaps in all odd-man-front zone defenses (1-3-1, 1-2-2, 3-2). It tries to split defenders with four outside players. The forwards and center continually roll and replace one another, looking for passes in the lane or low-post. By employing a hiding effect or approaching from behind the zone, players can take advantage of sudden openings within the heart of the defense. Meanwhile, the guards are used as passers or step-in jump shooters.

When to Use Split
Split thrives on odd-man-front zone defenses. Here's why.

Against a 1-3-1 defense the four offensive players facing the basket find and fill the open areas on the court, creating immediate match-up problems for the point, wing, and baseline defenders.

The guards position themselves on opposite sides of the court in the vicinity of the key, splitting the point and wing defenders. The forwards are stationed in opposite corners, forcing the wing and baseline defenders to make similar unpleasant decisions. Meanwhile, the center flashes from the low-block to the high-post. If not denied by the middle defender, the center becomes a major threat for a shot or a pass leading to a shot.

Split's roll-and-replace action by the forwards and center wreaks havoc on the defense. If the back of the zone comes out to play the pass to the forward, the center may be open rolling to the low-block. If the middle defender denies the roll by the center, the forward can pass back to the guard, who may find the weakside forward replacing in the lane. Should the guard elect to pass back to the other forward, the weakside forward may eventually work his way open for a low-block pass.

While this action takes place guards may find themselves open for step-in jump shots or drives. Opportunity jump shots, drives, and pull up jumpers are available for forwards covered by a lone baseline defender.

The 1-2-2 and 3-2 zones are attacked by guards splitting the point and wing defenders and forwards splitting the wing and baseline defenders. The defense faces a tough question: Who guards the center pointing the ball and the forwards flashing into the paint? If communication by defenders is poor the middle of the zone can be left virtually uncovered.

We have not used Split against combination defenses, but have found it comes in handy against match-ups. If players 3, 4, and 5 are guarded with man-to-man principles, Split's roll-and-replace action against the back line can create excellent scoring opportunities. Quick openings in the lane and one-on-one opportunities abound.

Personnel Requirements

In the Split continuity the point and shooting guards are interchangeable, with one provision. One of the guards should be able to split or gap the defense off the dribble and look to pass. The other guard is primarily a pass catcher and shooter.

The forwards also can play either side of the floor. But again, specific skills create specific opportunities. The shooting forward might be more inclined to take a jump shot or use his one-on-one skills facing the basket. The power forward probably will be more effective flashing into the lane for quick, high-percentage shots.

The center is the hub of the Split attack. Throughout this continuity the center is an excellent target as either a scorer or a passer. Size and timing are always important attributes for a center. In the Split continuity they are even more important.

Diagrams of Split

Diagram 4-1 illustrates the basic alignment of players against all zones with odd-man fronts (in this case, a 1-2-2). Either guard can initiate the offense by passing to the center coming up the lane or to the forward on the strong side.

As 1 dribbles into a split area, 5 points the ball by attacking from the rear of the zone. If 5 is open in the lane, he offers an immediate scoring threat. If he is open at the high-post, he can either score, pass to 3 as a scoring threat, or pass to 2, who may have a two-on-one advantage with 4.

Diagram 4-2: As 1 passes to 3, 5 cuts to the low-post looking for a scoring pass. Player 4 looks for rebounding position on the opposite block in the event that 3 has a one-on-one scoring opportunity or 5 has a shot in the low-post. Players 1 and 2 step into gaps for possible open jump shots.

Diagram 4-3: Should 3 return the ball to 1, the opposite forward, 4, flashes into an area that may open in the lane. If 1 is tightly guarded, he must be able to make an overhead or bounce pass to 4. Meanwhile, 5 has looped to the opposite low-block for an alley-oop pass from 1 or rebounding position.

Diagram 4-4: If 1 passes back to 3, 4 cuts down the lane for a scoring opportunity on a feed by 3.

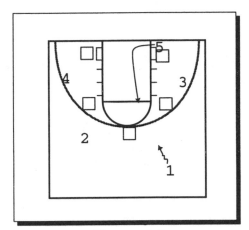

Diagram 4-1

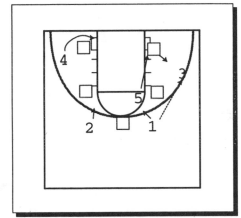

Diagram 4-2

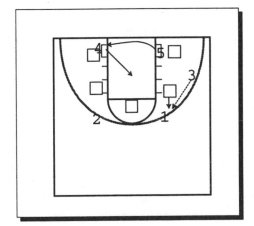

Diagram 4-3

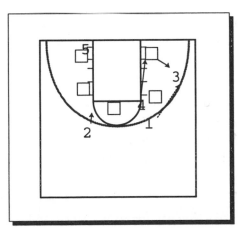

Diagram 4-4

Diagram 4-5: On a return pass from 3 to 1, 5 again flashes up the lane looking for a scoring opportunity or pointing the ball while 4 rolls across the lane.

Diagram 4-6: Whenever 1 elects to pass to the opposite guard, 2, 5 comes up the lane for a scoring opportunity or continues to point the ball at the high-post. Player 4 must loop back to his original position to give us a balanced 2-1-2 set.

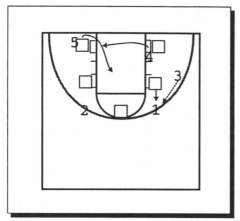

Diagram 4-5

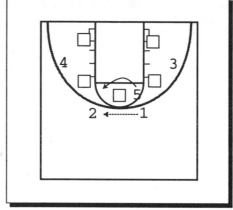

Diagram 4-6

Should 2 pass to 4, the same continuity of movement by players and ball occurs on the opposite side, with the same options illustrated in Diagrams 4-1 through 4-6.

Diagrams 4-7 through 4-11 show Split after its initiation against a 1-3-1 defense.

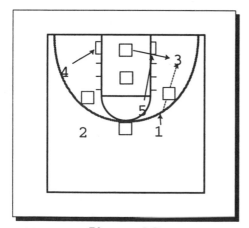

Diagram 4-7

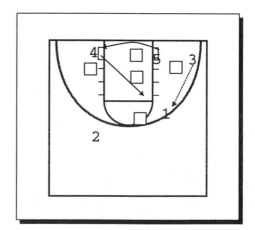

Diagram 4-8

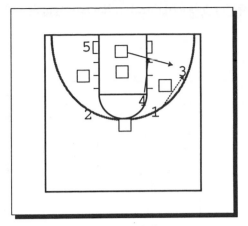

Diagram 4-9

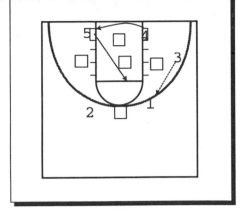

Diagram 4-10

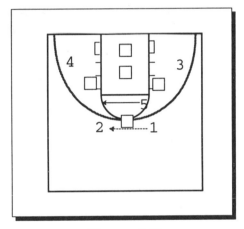

Diagram 4-11

Drills for Split

The following diagrams demonstrate the breakdown of Split by three offensive players (1, 4, and 5) and a coach (C). You can use three or four defenders to create a specific odd-man front.

• Diagram 4-12: As 1 dribbles to a split area, 5 comes up the lane as a scoring threat or continues to the high-post to point the ball. If 5 is not open, 1 passes to a coach, 5 rolls down the lane to the low-post for a scoring opportunity, and 4 moves to the weakside low-block for rebounding position.

• Diagram 4-13: When the coach returns a pass to 1, the opposite forward, 4, flashes into a gap in the lane or continues to the high-post to point the ball. Player 5 loops to the opposite block for an alley-oop pass from 1 or for rebounding position.

NOTE: This drill can be used on either side of the court to develop timing, passing, and scoring abilities.

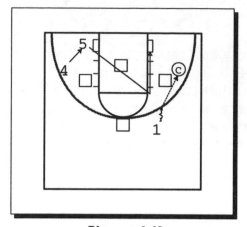

Diagram 4-12

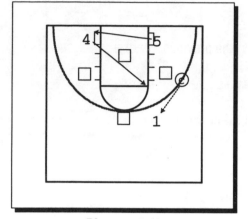

Diagram 4-13

CHAPTER 5

The Continuity 13

In the previous chapter we outlined a continuity, Split, that employs gap play against odd-man-front defenses (1-3-1,1-2-2, 3-2). The continuity 13 uses much the same gap play and roll-and-replace action to attack even-man-front defenses (2-3, 2-1-2). These two continuities effectively combat all the basic zones you'll see in a half-court setting. To take it a step further, they are just as effective should the defense be extended over any length of the court. Here we're only covering the half-court setting.

When to Use 13

The continuity 13 offers many excellent scoring opportunities against even-man-front defenses.

By using the short corner the power forward can gain an advantage for a shot, drive, or scoring pass. The wings, one of which is the scoring guard, become involved in the roll-and-replace action. If the point guard and the power forward are capable of executing the alley oop pass, you can surprise the back line of the zone with that demoralizing play.

Personnel Requirements

The point guard, 1, can be both a starter and a finisher in this continuity. First, he must create problems for the two-man defensive front by gapping the defenders off the dribble. Once the zone tips its hand and commits one way or the other the point guard must be able to swing the ball quickly to either side to take advantage of available openings. The center, 5, may be open in the lane, and the power forward, 4, may be open for an alley-oop pass.

This doesn't mean the point guard is solely a passer. If the down-the-middle shot is available the point guard can double as a zone-busting shooter.

The wings, 2 and 3, have many opportunities to shoot as they gap the guard and forward on their respective sides of the court. The wings should be able to drive into the gap occasionally, whether for a pull-up jump shot or for a pass to an open teammate. They should also be able to flash from the weak side into the lane for scoring opportunities.

The wings should be accomplished passers, since they will see many attractive openings for passes. The center is often open in the mid-post, the power forward in the low-post or short corner, and the point guard at the top of the key.

The power forward, 4, is essentially a baseline player who should have plenty of openings to shoot or drive from the short corner. He also flashes from block to block for post-up situations. Because at times the power forward flashes behind the defense, the power forward should be able to rise to the occasion for an alley-oop pass, usually from the point guard.

The center, 5, has responsibilities almost identical to those he faced in the continuity Split. Once again, the center is the hub of the offense and should be able to score or pass from the high-, mid-, or low-post areas.

Diagrams Of 13
As demonstrated in Diagram 5-1, 13 is a basic, 1-3-1 set formed by the point guard dribbling into the seam that appears at the top of the key in all even-man-front zones. The center, 5, attacks from the rear of the zone for a scoring opportunity in the lane or continues to the high-post to point the ball. If 5 receives a pass in the high-post he has several attractive options. Player 5 can try to score, can pass to 4 flashing in the lane, or can pass to either wing, 2 or 3, for scoring opportunities. Player 1 always has the option of looking for the alley-oop pass to 4, who positions himself beneath the block behind the zone. Players 2 and 3 are always in triple-threat position (jump shot, drive, or pass) when 1 or 5 has the ball.

Diagram 5-2: The wings station themselves in seams between the front and rear players in the zone. On a pass from 1 to 2, 4 flashes block-to-block for a possible lay-up or posting situation. If the back of the zone is forced to play 2 on the first pass, such an opportunity could present itself. Meanwhile, 5 always points the ball as an outlet.

If we had initiated the offense with a pass from 1 to 3, 4 would have stayed in the low-post for a scoring pass, 5 would have pointed the ball to the left side, and we still would be in our 1-3-1 set.

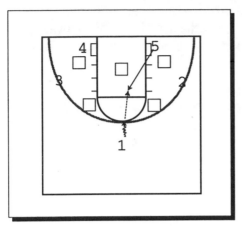

Diagram 5-1

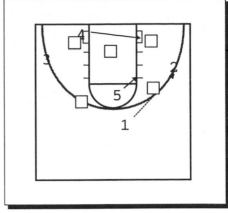

Diagram 5-2

Diagram 5-3: Player 4 pops out to the short corner facing the basket for a pass from 2 and a possible jump shot or drive. Player 5 rolls down the lane for a scoring pass from 4; 3 goes to the opposite low-block for rebounding position on a shot by 4 or 5. Players 1 and 2 step in for possible jump shots if the zone really collapses inside.

Diagram 5-4: On the return pass from 4 to 2, 5 loops across the lane to the opposite block, and 3 flashes across the lane into a gap created by the roll-and-replace action between 5 and 3.

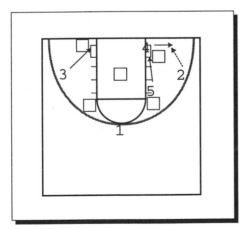

Diagram 5-3

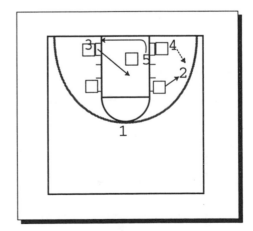

Diagram 5-4

Diagram 5-5: As the ball is reversed to the top of the key, 3 must loop quickly across the lane to his original position on the left side of the attack. Player 5 moves up the lane for a scoring opportunity or to point the ball; 4 returns to his original position beneath the block.

Diagram 5-6: Here's the same attack initiated to the left side. The same principles apply. Player 4 eventually moves to the short corner on the left side; 5 points the ball on that side of the court; 2 becomes a flashing player, taking on the role filled by 3 when the offense started opposite his wing.

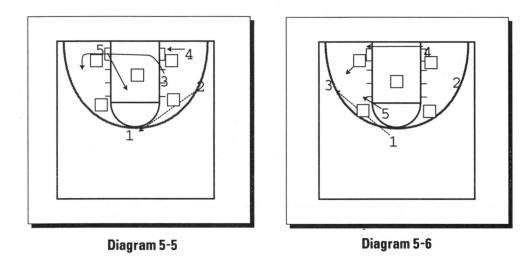

Diagram 5-5   **Diagram 5-6**

Diagrams 5-7 through 5-9 demonstrate continued action to the left side.

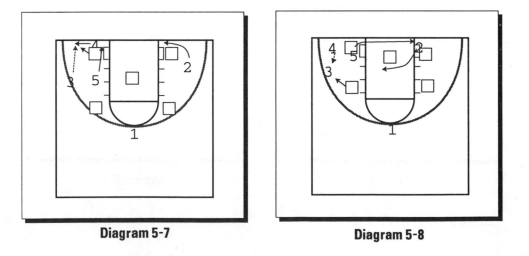

Diagram 5-7   **Diagram 5-8**

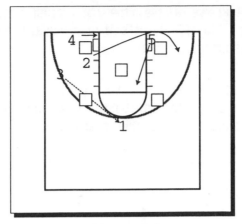

Diagram 5-9

Drills for 13

This drill for 13 involves three offensive players: a wing, 4, on the block and in the short corner, and a center, 5. Two coaches or a coach and a manager can simulate a point guard and a wing player. Employ as many defenders as you need to show the area of the zone you need to practice against.

• Diagram 5-10: Here, you're looking for the initiation and timing of the 1-3-1 attack. Player 5 looks for a scoring opportunity in the lane; 3 and a coach are in triple-threat positions; 4 looks for an alley-oop pass from the coach at the top of the key or is ready to flash should 5 receive a pass at the foul line.

• Diagram 5-11: On the pass from the coach to a wing, 4 works on flashing across the lane to a scoring position or the low-block, while 5 points the ball.

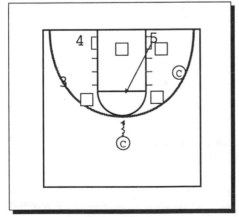

Diagram 5-10

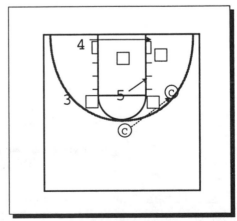

Diagram 5-11

• Diagram 5-12: Player 4 receives a pass in the short corner; 5 rolls to the low-block for a scoring pass from 4. Player 3, the offside wing, moves to the low-block opposite the ball for rebounding position.

• Diagram 5-13: On the return pass from the short corner to the wing, the opposite wing, 3, flashes into the lane, then to the ballside low block. Player 5 loops out of the lane to the opposite block for rebounding position.

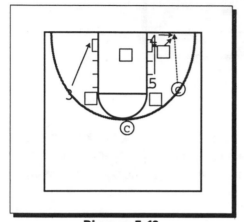
Diagram 5-12

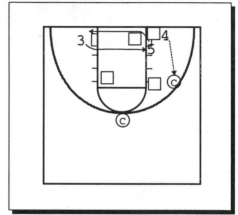
Diagram 5-13

• Diagram 5-14: On the pass to the top of the key, 5 comes up the lane for a scoring opportunity or to point the ball; 3 loops across the lane to his original wing position; and 4 moves to the low block for a possible alley-oop pass.

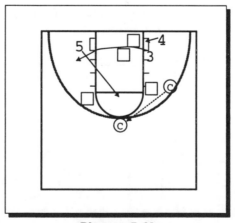
Diagram 5-14

NOTE: By repeating this drill to the right side we develop timing, passing, and scoring opportunities. We can easily switch this drill to the left side by switching the coach from one side to the other and starting 2 in his original position.

CHAPTER 6

The Continuity BC

BC takes its name from Brookland-Cayce High School in Columbia, South Carolina, where George Beam coached a very successful program. We have taken his basic principles against all zones and, by using interior screens, have found that we can get the ball inside. When running BC a smart coach interchanges frontline players according to their skills. Certain players set strong screens while others are more comfortable using screens. BC gives a coach flexibility in defining players' roles.

One key element of BC is a screener's ability to spin back into openings in the mid-post area.

When to Use BC

BC works best against the 3-2, 1-2-2, and 1-3-1 zones, some combination zones, and match-ups.

The 3-2 and 1-2-2 zones offer a very similar defensive look, with only two defenders stationed near the basket. BC tries to exploit that essential weakness. The initial pass forces one back-line defender to go to the corner. Once that happens the offense screens the other back-line defender, creating openings on the low block.

In the 3-2 zone, a back-line defender faces tremendous responsibilities. When the ball is on his side of the court, a back-line defender must choose between covering a jump shooter in the corner or an attacking player on the low block. When the ball is in the opposite corner, the back-line defender must cover the low-post on that side of the court. With good ball movement and screens the BC offense makes the back-line defender's job of covering three areas all the more difficult.

In the 1-3-1 zone problems arise for the middle defender if he must move from the foul line or center of the lane to the low block. If the BC offense forces the back-line defender to cover a jump shooter in the corner, the middle defender must cut off the low-post area on the ballside. If he is back-picked or up-picked, the middle defender faces a difficult task even getting to the low-post area, much less defending against an offensive player flashing into that prime scoring area.

Against combinations, we have had particular success if player 3 or 4 is being played man-to-man. Let's say the defense is a box-and-one or diamond-and-one and the player being covered one-on-one is player 3 or 4. The BC's screening action concentrates on the one-on-one defender, creating openings in the low-post and mid-post areas. The four other attacking players also enjoy numerous openings.

If the defense is a triangle-and-two and either or both the 3 and 4 players face one-on-one coverage, the screens and natural movement of the BC offense create openings.

Against match-ups, which have much in common with regular man-to-man defenses, the BC is a natural. Player 2, by running from corner to corner, presents problems for the defense whenever he runs under the basket and pops out to the corner for a potential jump shot. Who covers him?

Players 3 and 4 rotate into the post area by a series of screens across, upscreens, and downscreens. Player 5 becomes a major threat on the spinback move as defenders try to communicate and switch assignments on screens. Meanwhile, player 1 picks his spots for jump shots, some one-on-one play, and passing options.

Although the 2-3 zone takes away the inside game more often than not, we don't rule out the BC. The secondary action and ball reversal can get the ball to the low- or mid-post, and step-in jump shots are available when the defense collapses.

Personnel Requirements

Player 1, the point guard, has the vital responsibility of initiating the offense, especially if we want to score on our first screen or spinback. Player 1 must take the dribble away from the side of the court he wants to attack, then quickly reverse direction and dribble right at the defender he wants to guard him. By occupying one defender in this fashion, 1 forces a back-line defender to guard the shooting guard, who receives a pass in the corner. On return passes from the corner 1 must be able to hit a jump shot, pass to teammates in the lane or mid-post area, or quickly reverse the ball.

The shooting guard's first responsibility is part of his title—shoot the ball if open and be a threat from either corner. Upon receiving the initial pass 2 has the option of shooting, passing to the low-post, or passing to the mid-post. Player 2's first look is to player 3 or 4 approaching the low-post from the baseline. Next, 2 looks to the mid-post, where 5 has spun back after setting his initial screen. Player 2 must move quickly from corner to corner and be in triple-threat position upon receiving a pass. Player 2 can also rebound if he elects to follow his own shots.

Players 3 and 4 have the same basic responsibilities once the ball goes from one side of the court to the other. They must be good flash players to the low- and mid-post areas and have the ability to be weak side rebounders. When facing the basket their main responsibility is swinging the pass to the corner.

Player 5, the center, should have the size it takes to set effective screens across or up the lane. After setting those screens he must spin back to the ball as a scoring or passing threat. Since 5 basically stays within ten feet of the basket he should always be in position to rebound.

Diagrams of BC

Diagram 6-1 shows the basic alignment of BC, should the continuity be run to the right side. The point guard, 1, dribbles to occupy the right-side defender in an even-man-front zone or the wing defender on that side of an odd-man-front zone. In BC, the shooting guard, 2, has scoring and passing responsibilities in both corners. The center, 5, is basically a screener who may use spinback action to create scoring opportunities. Players 3 and 4 are interchangeable, with many of the same responsibilities.

Here's the screening action against even-man-front zones (2-3, 2-1-2). When the initial pass from 1 to 2 is in flight, 5 screens the middle player in the rear of the zone, then spins back to a mid-post area for a scoring opportunity. Player 5 is screening for 4, who usually goes baseline. By going baseline, 4 attacks from the rear of the zone, giving 5 the opportunity to spin back to an opening in the mid-post area.

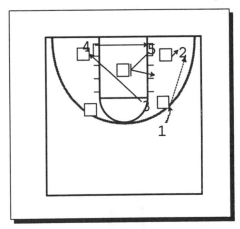

Diagram 6-1

This ideal situation is set up in large part by the guards. If 1 can occupy a defender in the front of the zone, the rear defender on that side must be alert for a pass to 2 in the corner. Once the pass is made from 1 to 2, the rear defender must defend against the possible corner jump shot. Once that occurs, 5's screen on the middle defender should free 4 for a low-post scoring opportunity.

On the pass to the corner, 3 moves diagonally across the lane for rebounding position on the low-block.

Diagram 6-2: Once the ball moves to the corner, most zones, no matter what their initial alignment, fall into a 2-3 pattern to take away the corner jump shot, post play on the strong side, and rebounding and alley-oop possibilities on the weak side.

On the return pass from 2 to 1 a number of cuts and screens occur. Player 4 must x-out to the elbow area on the flight of 2's pass to 1; 2 immediately runs the baseline to the opposite corner. The next screen usually opens a gap in the lane because the middle defender in any zone is recovering to deny passes in his area. After 4 x's out, 5 sets a downscreen against the middle player in what has become a 2-3 zone. This allows 3 to pick his open shot in the gap in the lane. Player 1 helps to create the gap by forcing a player in the front of the zone to play him. After 5 sets a screen on a baseline defender, he moves across the lane to the opposite block.

Diagram 6-3: Player 3 slides down the lane if he didn't receive a pass in the middle; 1 passes to 4.

NOTE: Setting legal screens and avoiding three-second violations are musts in order for this continuity to work.

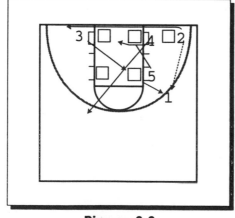

Diagram 6-2

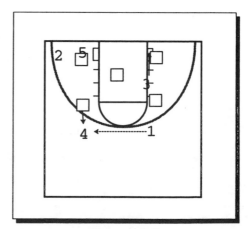

Diagram 6-3

Diagram 6-4: The ball is reversed from 1 to 4 to 2. On the pass to 2 the same attack begins on the left side of the court. Having read what type of zone the defense is playing on our initial attack, 5 screens the appropriate player, as the zone will be the same on ball reversal. Player 3 is now the player using the screen to go baseline, allowing 5 a good spinback opening in the mid-post. Player 4 moves diagonally across the lane to the opposite low-block for rebounding position. Player 1 fills the area vacated by 4 for an outlet pass.

Diagram 6-5: On the pass from 2 to 1, 3 x's out to the elbow, and 2 goes baseline to the opposite corner. Player 5 sets a downscreen on the middle man in the rear of the zone, allowing 4 to cut to a gap in the lane.

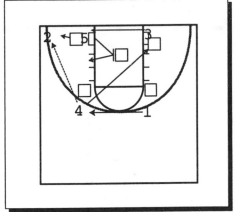

Diagram 6-4

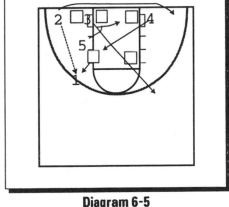

Diagram 6-5

Diagram 6-6: On ball reversal 5 has set his screen and continued across the lane to the ballside low-post. If 4 doesn't receive a pass in the lane he continues to the low-block opposite the ball. The offense is initiated again with a pass by 3 to the corner and screening action by 5 and 4.

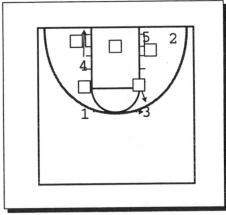

Diagram 6-6

Diagrams 6-7 through 6-12 show BC against a 1-2-2 defense. Diagrams 6-13 through 6-18 show BC against a 1-3-1 defense.

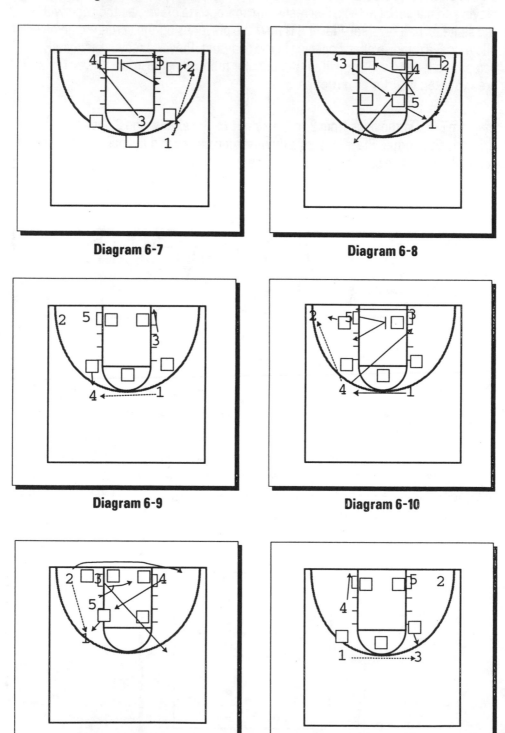

Diagram 6-7

Diagram 6-8

Diagram 6-9

Diagram 6-10

Diagram 6-11

Diagram 6-12

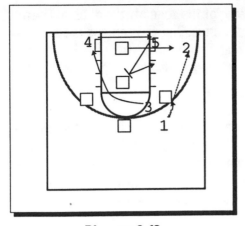

Diagram 6-13

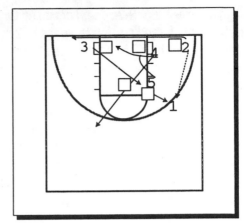

Diagram 6-14

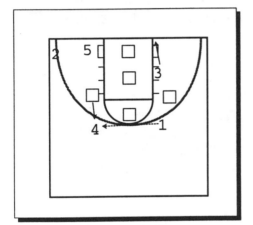

Diagram 6-15

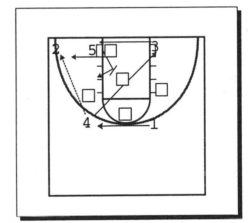

Diagram 6-16

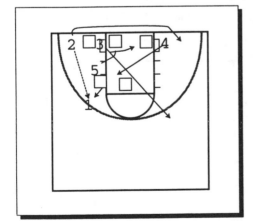

Diagram 6-17

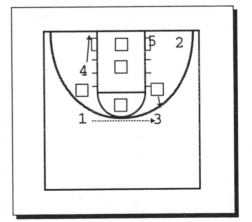

Diagram 6-18

Against a 1-2-2 or 3-2 zone, 1 occupies the wing of the zone off the dribble. The rear defender is forced to play the pass to 2 in the corner. Player 5 screens the other rear defender on the flight of the pass to the corner. Player 5 then spins back to the middle for a scoring opportunity, while 3 moves diagonally across the lane to the opposite block.

Against a 1-3-1 zone 1 occupies the wing of the zone off the dribble, forcing the rear defender to play the pass to 2 in the corner. Player 5 screens the middle player in the zone on the flight of the pass to the corner; 5's screen could be described as an up-pick or a back-pick. Either way, the goal is to free 4 on the low block. Player 5 then spins back to the mid-post for a scoring opportunity, while 3 moves to the opposite low-block.

NOTE: Players 1 and 2 will find open jump shots should the perimeter defenders be more concerned with helping out against inside players. If 1 and 2 step in, high-percentage jump shots do develop.

Drills for BC
• Diagram 6-19: Here's a drill to develop good screening and spinback action by 5 and use of the screen by 4 for a low-post scoring opportunity. Player 2 works on his passing skills to the low-post or mid-post. Players 4 and 5 receive passes in the gut of the zone and work on their scoring and rebounding skills. Three defenders can simulate the rear of a 2-3, 2-1-2, 3-2, or 1-3-1 zone. Here we show the back line of a 2-3 defense.

• Diagram 6-20: A coach has the ball in the corner facing three defenders simulating the back line of a zone. On the pass from a coach or manager to 1, the coach or manager on the low-block Xs out and 5 screens the middle player in the rear of the zone. Player 1 tries to hit 3 flashing into a gap in the lane.

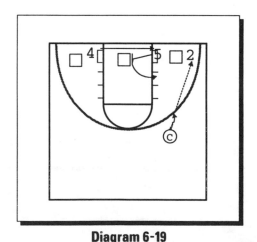

Diagram 6-19

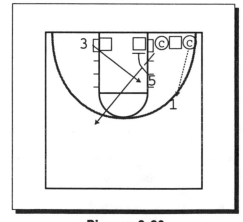

Diagram 6-20

• Diagram 6-21: Here's the movement of 5 and 3 if a pass doesn't go into the lane.

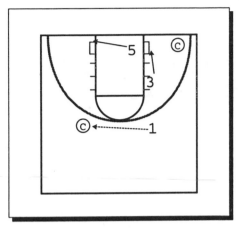

Diagram 6-21

NOTE: Both drills emphasize timing and the players' passing, screening, and scoring abilities. The harder the defenders work, the more effective your offense becomes. We work on initiating these drills on both sides of the court.

CHAPTER 7

The Continuity Blue

I have found that defenses are particularly vulnerable when quick overloads force defenders to make a difficult choice. Blue, which can be used against any zone defense, is a true power game. By using quick overloads and an x-out effect by our power forward and center, we create good passing angles for our guards, should they be tightly covered. An open jump shot or one-on-one opportunity for the opposite guard is always an option.

When to Use Blue
The 2-3 zone defense probably combats the Blue continuity better than other zones, but it is still vulnerable. Four offensive players outnumber three defenders in a quick overload situation. The ballside guard, ballside forward, and middle defender in the 2-3 zone have problems if not helped by the offside guard and offside forward.

In attacking the 3-2 and 1-2-2 defenses, the Blue continuity forces defenders to make difficult decisions regarding who will cover the short corner, low-post, and mid-post. Another question: On ball reversal who defends the lane when the power forward and center use x-out action?

Against a 1-3-1 defense the Blue continuity creates primary scoring opportunities in the short corner, low-post, and mid-post. Many open shots are available in the short corner should the baseline defender rush out to cover the shooting guard on the first pass.

Personnel Requirements
The point guard, 1, starts the attack by dribbling away from the side to be overloaded. The zone usually shifts with the ball and the dribble, enabling the point guard to catch the defense by surprise and create an overload when he changes direction. Once the overload is achieved, the point guard can pass to the short corner and the low- and mid-post or can find an occasional open jump shot should the defense sag.

The shooting guard, 2, attacks the defense from behind for a shot in the wing area. His primary passing outlets are the short corner and the low- and mid-post areas.

The small forward, 3, also attacks the zone from behind for a short corner shot or a pass to the low- and mid-post areas. On ball reversal, 3 cuts from corner to corner behind the defense. With four players on one side of the floor openings for drives aren't generally available. However, since 3 is stationed close to the basket, he often finds inside-out rebounding opportunities. In other words, he is in position to employ many of the same box-out principles he might use on the defensive end.

The power forward, 4, screens for the shooting guard and shooting forward, then posts up on the low-block. On ball reversal, 4's x-out action with the center creates shots in the lane or mid-post areas. Rebounding is a must.

The center, 5, starts at the high post, then moves from the mid-post to the low-post on x-out action. He has many of the same responsibilities as the power forward. Both players should be able to score, pass, and rebound from their areas.

Diagrams of Blue

Diagram 7-1 shows the initial alignment of players attacking a 2-3 zone. By moving forwards 3 and 4 to the opposite side of the floor and 2 and 5 in the same manner, the play can be run on the left side.

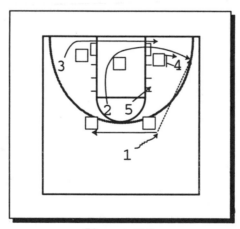

Diagram 7-1

The point guard, 1, dribbles right to occupy a guard on that side of an even-man-front zone or a wing player in an odd-man-front zone. A quick overload is created when 4 sets a screen on the back of the zone, 2 cuts, and 3 follows 2 to the short corner. A defender must choose between guarding 2 or 3. Both are facing the basket; both can hit the jump shot.

When 2 receives the pass he can try to score, or he has four options, depending on how the defense reacts to the initial overload. Player 3 may be open for a jump shot or a baseline drive; 4 posts up on the low-block; 5 is at the high-post. A crosscourt pass to 1 may create a jump shot or a one-on-one opportunity if the defense elects to match up man-to-man on the right side. The various options should 2 pass to 3, 4, or 5 are obvious, according to how the defense plays the next pass.

Diagrams 7-2 and 7-3: If the pass from 2, 3, 4, or 5 goes crosscourt to 1, or if 2 dribbles toward 1 to create a passing lane, the next diagrams show how an overload quickly develops a power game on the left side. On the flight of the pass to 1, 5 Xs from the high-post to the low-post, looking for an opening or setting a screen on the rear of the zone. Player 4 Xs high after 5 cuts and looks for a scoring or passing opportunity at the high-post. Player 3 goes short corner to short corner looking for a baseline score. When 1 receives the pass, he has an immediate scoring opportunity or the same four options 2 had on the initial pass to the right side.

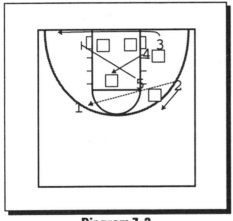

Diagram 7-2

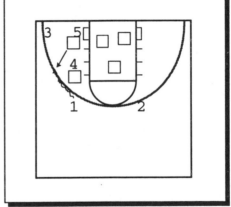

Diagram 7-3

Diagram 7-4: On a ball reversal back to the right side, where 2 is isolated, the same cuts and screens are implemented to create the original overload.

Diagram 7-5 through 7-7 show the Blue continuity against a 1-2-2 defense. Diagrams 7-8 through 7-10 show Blue against a 1-3-1 defense.

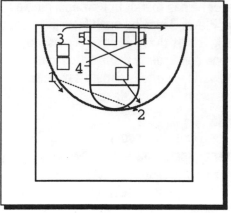

Diagram 7-4

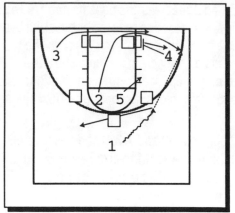

Diagram 7-5

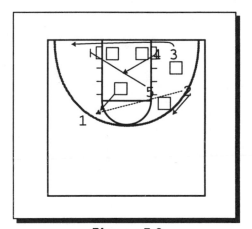

Diagram 7-6

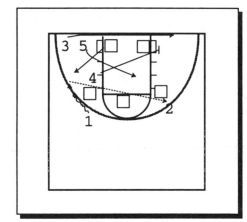

Diagram 7-7

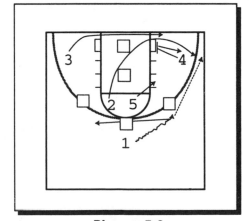

Diagram 7-8

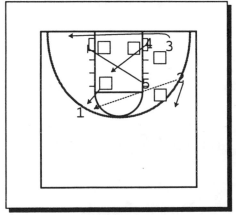

Diagram 7-9

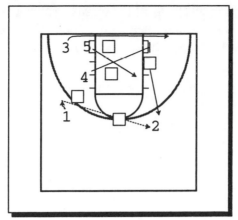

Diagram 7-10

Drills for Blue

• Diagram 7-11: In drilling the Blue continuity, we have found it best to use 3, 4, and 5 as the offensive players trying to score, with two coaches or a coach and a manager just passing and moving the ball appropriately. Basically, we will exploit the baseline of a zone defense for open jump shots or for one-on-one scoring opportunities. The coach determines how many defenders are on the floor and just what type of defense they're playing. On offense we're trying to improve the timing, passing, and scoring skills of 3, 4, and 5. In this diagram, a coach initiates the offense by dribbling to the right. Cutters C and 3 use a screen set by 4.

• Diagram 7-12: On the pass to the coach simulating 2, passes to 3, 4, and 5 are our first choices. If they can get a high-percentage shot off that particular pass or need to follow with the next pass and a better shot, we try to develop that aspect of the continuity.

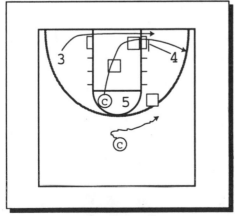

Diagram 7-11

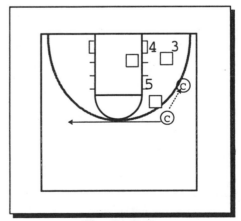

Diagram 7-12

• Diagram 7-13: On ball reversal by any of the offensive players to the weak side coach, 5 and 4 work on the timing of their x-out action. Also, 5 and 1 work on using screens. Again, the coach looks for the appropriate pass for a scoring situation.

• Diagram 7-14 is a continuation for an overload on the right side and scoring opportunities there.

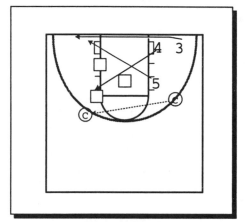

Diagram 7-13

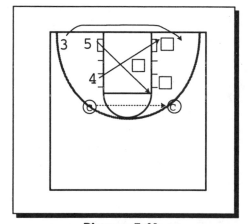

Diagram 7-14

CHAPTER 8

The Continuity Special

After losing our 1982 conference championship game to South Carolina-Spartanburg, the eventual NAIA champion, we felt we needed to attack 1-3-1 zones better. In Special, we start in a 2-1-2 formation similar to Split, but attack the baseline instead of concentrating on roll-and-replace action. An open jump shot or a one-on-one opportunity for the opposite guard is always an option.

When to Use Special

Special starts as a high 2-3 versus regular zones or half-court traps. The continuity works particularly well against 1-3-1 defenses, which are vulnerable to low triangles formed on the baseline. Quick passes create and exploit overloads before the defense can adjust.

Special also works against 2-3, 3-2, and 1-2-2 zones. It is quite simple to teach, overloads zones well, and creates its share of mid-post jump shots and offside-guard jump shots.

We do not use Special against match-ups or combination defenses. It is simply too stationary to attack such defenses effectively.

When attacking a 1-3-1 zone it is important to use the weakside forward moving to the block or short corner. By forcing the baseline defender to cover the strong-side forward and screening the middle player in the zone, Special creates openings on the low block. If the middle player guards the low-block, who covers the weakside forward should he continue to the short corner? On a quick pass the 15-foot jump shot is available for the short corner. Should the middle defender take away that option, the attacking player in the mid-post area rolls down the lane for an excellent scoring opportunity.

Against a 2-3 zone, Special creates many of the same problems for defenders, especially if a defender is pulled out to match up with the attacking forward on the strong side. The low block usually is not open, but the short corner is often available because the middle defender has such a long way to travel. Should the short-corner player be covered by the middle defender, the attacking player at the mid-post usually has an excellent scoring opportunity if he is not picked up immediately by the weakside forward.

A 3-2 or 1-2-2 defense also faces tough decisions about guarding the strong-side forward, the short corner and the center rolling to the basket.

Personnel Requirements

The guards, 1 and 2, have similar roles in this continuity. Either can initiate the offense to his side of the court, with three potential outlets: the strong-side forward, the mid-post player, and the weakside guard.

Both guards should be able to step in for the jump shot in the gap. If the zone starts wide or widens out, both guards will have opportunities to penetrate and outnumber the defense.

The forwards, 3 and 4, also play interchangeable roles. If the ball is brought to his side a forward must be enough of a threat to draw a back line defender out to guard him.

Passing options include the other forward flashing to the low-post, the center in the mid-post area, and either guard stepping in for a jump shot.

If the opposite guard has the ball, a forward must start on the weakside low block, then, on a pass to the other forward, must flash block-to-block, for a post-up situation. If the low-post option is well guarded the forward must move quickly to the short corner to create an opening for the center.

The center, 5, points the ball, whether it's in the hands of a guard on the perimeter or a forward in the short corner. High-post and mid-post jump shots are available, as are low-post opportunities should the ball be in the short corner. A pass to the weak side is always available.

Diagrams of Special

Diagram 8-1 shows the initiation of Special to the right side of the court. The offense can be initiated just as easily to the left side by passing to 2 or 4. The offense can also be initiated by a pass to the center, 5, who then passes back to the guard. With that initiation, you automatically find yourself in the second phase of the offense.

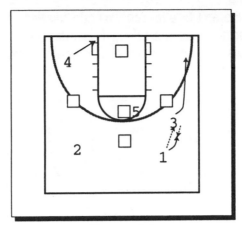

Diagram 8-1

After 3 returns the ball to 1, he moves to an area that forces the rear man in the zone to play him. Against a 1-3-1 half-court trap, the return pass from 3 to 1 finds 1 closer to mid-court. However, the same principles and movement still apply.

Notice that on the first pass to 3, 4 has gone to the opposite block for an alley-oop pass or rebounding position.

Diagram 8-2: On the second pass from 1 to 3, 5 screens the middle player in the defense, then spins back to a mid-post area. Player 4 flashes across the lane to the low block. Again, an important aspect of the second pass to 3 is that a rear player in the zone must dart out to defend against 3. With or without the screen by 5, there is the possibility of a two-on-one situation for 4 and 5. If the ball is reversed 2 may be open for a jump shot or one-on-one drive.

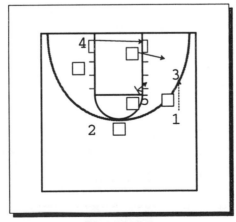

Diagram 8-2

Diagram 8-3: If 4 and 5 aren't free for scoring opportunities, 4 can break out to the short corner for a jump shot or a short drive if no defender guards him. If the defender quickly guards 4, 5 cuts down the lane for a lay-up or low-post scoring opportunity.

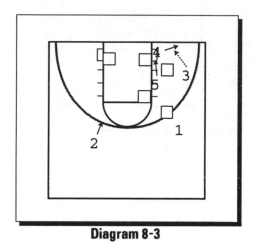

Diagram 8-3

NOTE: The triangle overloads created by 3, 4, and 5 and 1, 3, and 5 can be explored with any number of passes before the ball is reversed to the opposite side of the court.

Diagram 8-4: Once the ball is reversed to the weak side from 1 to 2, try to develop quick overloads and triangles on the left side. Player 5 moves directly across the court to the mid-post; 4 loops to the forward position hoping to draw the rear of the zone to him should he receive a pass.

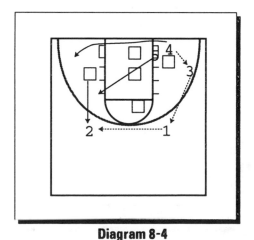

Diagram 8-4

Diagram 8-5: On the pass to 4, 5 backpicks a middle defender in a 1-3-1 or 2-1-2 zone, then spins back to the mid-post area. Player 3 quickly flashes across the lane to the low-post area, creating a triangle with 4 and 5 and a possible overload situation. Player 1 remains available for a jump shot or drive.

Diagram 8-6: If 3 breaks to the short corner he may be open for a jump shot or drive on a pass from 2. If 3 is guarded tightly, he looks to 5 sliding down the lane for a lay-up or low-post scoring opportunity.

On quick ball reversal back to the right side try to create triangles for open jump shots, posting, or drives.

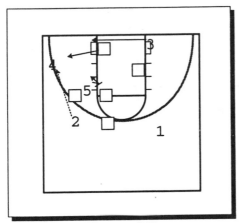

Diagram 8-5

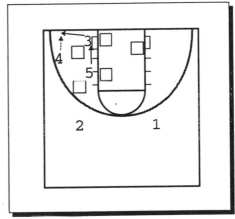

Diagram 8-6

Drills for Special

• Diagram 8-7: Set the defense accordingly and work on the timing of passes and cuts by a coach or manager and 3, 4, and 5. Here, we're working against a simulated 1-3-1 defense.

• Diagram 8-8: On the second pass from a coach to 3, 5 backpicks the middle player in the zone, then spins back to the mid-post, while 4 flashes directly across the lane.

• Diagram 8-9: Player 4 breaks to the short corner for a jump shot, drive, or pass to 5 sliding down the lane.

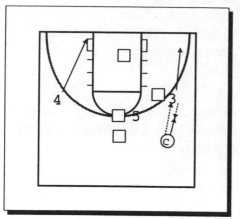

Diagram 8-7

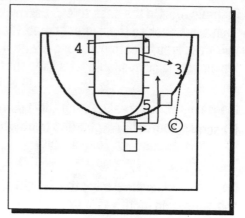

Diagram 8-8

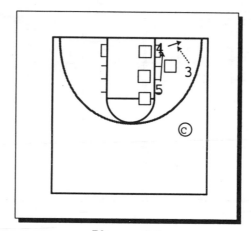

Diagram 8-9

CHAPTER 9

The Continuity Gold

By screening the rear of a zone defense and throwing skip passes you can create uncontested corner jump shots for your guards. Meanwhile, two post players constantly look for the ball inside.

When to Use Gold

This continuity is extremely effective against a 1-2-2 or 3-2 zone and even more potent against a 1-3-1, because it screens the area of the zone that must react to prevent open corner jump shots. Skip passes force defenders to sprint out, but effective screens prevent them from doing so. Should the defender successfully sprint to cover the jump shooter, low-post scoring opportunities are available for your big players.

Against a 3-2 or 1-2-2 defense we try to surprise the back of the zone by screening for our guards, who are on the move to the corners. By using the elbow-to-corner skip pass or quick elbow-to-elbow-to-corner ball reversal, the guards are isolated in the corners, or low-post opportunities present themselves. Double duck-in action is a problem for the two defenders in the back of the zone, as is a diagonal cut from the low-post to the high-post. Also, as the back of the zone rushes out to cover the guards in the corners, it is difficult for the opposite low player to come across the lane to deny a pass to the screener posting up.

When attacking a 1-3-1 defense we try to screen the lone defender in the rear of the zone, as it is usually this player's responsibility to cover a potential jump shooter in the corner. If a wing defender moves to cover the corner we screen him initially. Many times, a guard is stationed as the lone back-line defender in a 1-3-1 defense. Guards—or any smaller players—are vulnerable to screening action by taller, stronger frontline players. Double duck-in action can be very effective, especially if the wings play wide.

Although at times we have used the Gold continuity against 2-3 zones, it is much more difficult screening a three-player back line than it is to screen two players (3-2 or 1-2-2) or one player (1-3-1).

We do not run this continuity against match-up or combination defenses.

Personnel Requirements

The guards, 1 and 2, should be good corner shooters with the ability to feed a screener posting up.

The forwards, 3 and 4, and the center, 5, have the same responsibilities in this attack. They are screeners, post-up players, and flashing players. They must be able to feed their post-up or double duck-in counterparts for high-percentage shots.

Diagrams of Gold

The Gold continuity, shown in the following diagrams against a 1-2-2 zone, begins as a 2-3 set but quickly becomes a 2-1-2 in Diagram 9-1. The forward, 4, points the ball on the dribble by 2. If you feel you can get a quick scoring thrust on your first pass or two, switch your best scorers and screeners at the start.

Diagram 9-2: Player 2 passes to 1, then fades to the corner as 5 screens the rear of the zone on that side. Player 4 steps out to face the basket; 3 moves to a mid-post area.

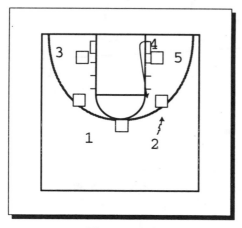

Diagram 9-1

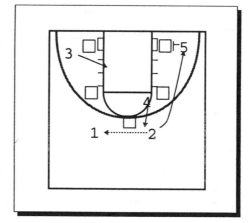

Diagram 9-2

Diagram 9-3: Player 1 has three potential passes. If the pass is made to 4, 4 looks for 2, who is using a screen by 5. Should this occur, 2 looks for a shot or feeds the ball to 5, who has moved into the low-post after screening for 2. Other options include passes to 3 or 4 ducking into gaps in the defense.

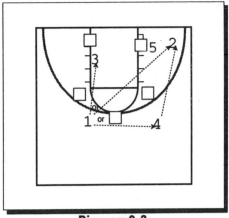

Diagram 9-3

Diagrams 9-4 and 9-5: On ball reversal from 2 to 4 to 1, or if 2 never receives a pass and the ball is reversed from 4 to 1, cuts and exchanges occur. Player 3 pops out to the corner; 5 flashes diagonally up the lane for a gap play; and 4 and 2 exchange, with 4 going to the low-block.

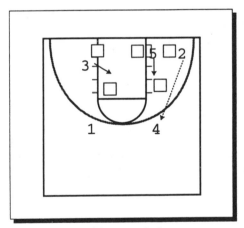

Diagram 9-4

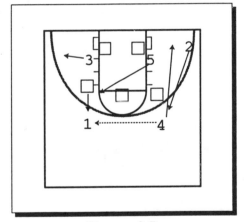

Diagram 9-5

Diagram 9-6: When 1 reverses the ball to 2, 3 sets a screen on the rear of the zone, and 1 fades to the corner. Player 4 steps into the lane for a mid-post scoring opportunity, and 5 steps out as an outlet.

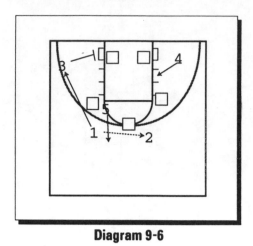

Diagram 9-6

Diagrams 9-7 through 9-12 show the Gold continuity against a 1-3-1 defense.

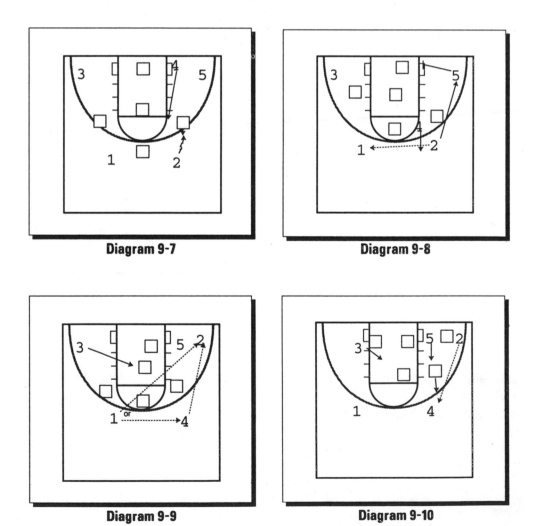

Diagram 9-7

Diagram 9-8

Diagram 9-9

Diagram 9-10

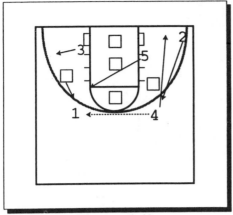

Diagram 9-11

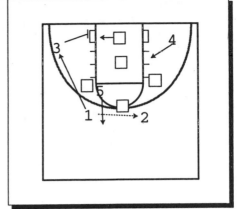

Diagram 9-12

Drills for Gold

• Diagram 9-13: Player 2 passes to a coach or manager; 5 sets a screen on the rear of the zone for 2 fading to the corner; and 4 steps out to a position facing the basket.

• Diagram 9-14: The options are a crosscourt pass to 2 for a jump shot or dump-in feed to 5 and a pass to 4. Player 4 then looks for 2 in the corner or for 5 posting up after setting a screen.

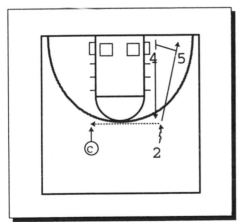

Diagram 9-13

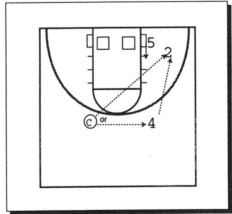

Diagram 9-14

CHAPTER 10

Set Plays: The Red Series

Having diagrammed and discussed the six continuities, it's time to move on to their logical alternative: set plays. Altogether, we have 10 set plays. The first seven (Red, Fade, Middle, Comeback, Go, Dribble Block, and Philly) are all part of the Red Series described in this chapter. The other three (Carolina, Away, and Away 3) are lob plays. We'll address them as a group in Chapter 11.

The Red Series takes its name from former Yeshiva University Basketball Coach Red Sarachek. While Yeshiva is not known as a basketball power, Sarachek is a student of the game and has studied many of the principles used in the Red Series.

All Red Series plays originate in a 1-3-1 set. From that basic set all players cut, fill, and screen with ball movement. The Red Series offers two immediate advantages. Because all seven plays are variations of one series, there's plenty of deception involved. Also, Red Series plays are effective against a variety of zones, including match-ups and combinations.

Running these plays to both sides of the court adds variety and flexibility to your set-play attacks.

When to Use Set Plays

While continuities are designed to create openings for all players, set plays create opportunities for specified shooters. Maybe you want to go with a certain player while he has a hot hand. Maybe you like a certain player in end-game, pressure-cooker situations. Set plays create the chances your top gun needs to do his thing.

Although the seven Red Series plays can be used against virtually all zone defenses and even against man-to-man defenses, certain plays work better against certain zones. For example, we use Red against all zones because it does a good job creating overloads involving our shooting guard.

Fade is more effective against 1-3-1 or 1-2-2 zones because its effectiveness is based in large part on screening a defender in the back of the zone. In the 1-3-1 there is only one such defender. In the 1-2-2 there are only two. Comeback also is best against 1-3-1 and 1-2-2 zones for many of the same reasons.

Middle is particularly effective against 1-2-2 zones and may be effective against 2-3 zones because both present large openings in the lane. Conversely, 1-3-1 and 2-1-2 defenses tend to eliminate those openings.

Philly and Go also thrive against 1-2-2 or 2-3 defenses for many of the same reasons. In Go we try to get the ball into the middle with the help of a screen. Dribble Block, on the other hand, is most effective versus 2-1-2 or 2-3 zones.

All seven Red Series plays are good against match-up zone defenses because of all the movement involved in running them. Red Series plays may also be effective against combination defenses. Red, Fade, Comeback, and Dribble Block effectively isolate a shooting guard off a cut or pick. Should the shooting guard or interchangeable small forward be guarded man-to-man, this type of offensive action can help him shake free.

Personnel Requirements

The point guard, 1, is primarily a passer and ballhandler with limited shooting responsibilities. The point guard must initiate the offense as tightly as possible to reduce the need for long, interceptable passes. If a set play is stymied, the point guard must have the presence of mind and communications skills to get the team into its breakdown offense. He also must be in position to protect the backcourt defensively.

The shooting guard, 2, is ideally a mobile, long-range weapon. He moves more than any other player in our set play offense, and therefore needs quickness and speed. Once the shooting guard gets to the designated payoff area, he must be able to hit perimeter shots. Ability to use screens, to penetrate, and to pass makes for a more complete shooting guard.

The small forward, 3, can be interchanged with the shooting guard if he is a proficient shooter. He also can switch places with the power forward, 4, and play with his back to the basket. The small forward must be a good passer.

The power forward, 4, should be able to score or pass from the low-post or flashing into the lane. He also should have the ability to set a screen, then post-up for a scoring opportunity.

The center, 5, shares many responsibilities with the power forward. He also must be a threat to score or pass from the high post. His accessibility as a target for passes is a must.

Diagrams of Set Plays: Red
In this section, the use of Red against 2-1-2, 1-2-2, and 1-3-1 defenses is discussed.

Diagram 10-1 shows the basic formation of Red against a 2-1-2 defense. Player 4 points the ball at the foul line and 1 advances the ball to the top of the key. If you want to start the play to the left side, switch 2 with 3 and 4 with 5. If you want 3 cutting from one side of the floor to the other, he can easily play 2's role.

NOTE: All Red Series plays end at the completion of a specific scoring opportunity. At that point, the most effective offense to enter is 13 or Split. The reason is simple. At the college level you must deal with a shot clock. The transition to 13 or Split is fairly easy and both attacks quickly produce high-percentage shots.

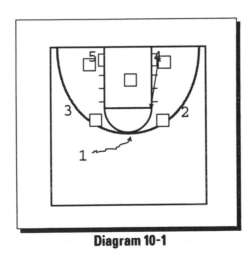

Diagram 10-1

Diagram 10-2: If 1 can pass to 2, he does so, then cuts behind 2 for a hand-off. Player 2 then cuts behind the defense to the other side of the floor and looks for a gap in the zone. If the defense denies a pass to 2, 1 sends him on a cut to the other side of the court by dribbling to 2's area instead of risking a potential turnover pass.

Once 2 cuts, 4 follows him to the short corner on the other side of the floor. After 4 has vacated the high-post area, 5 flashes diagonally into the lane looking for a scoring opportunity or trying to point the ball. Player 3 moves slightly to his right for an outlet pass.

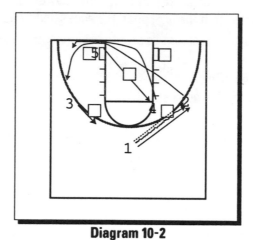

Diagram 10-2

Diagram 10-3: On ball reversal 3 must occupy the guard on his side of a two-man-front zone or the wing in a 1-2-2 or 3-2 zone. This creates a potential two-on-one scoring opportunity for 2 and 4 on a pass to 2. Player 2 can take a jump shot, drive into a gap and penetrate, or make a well-timed pass to 4 for a jump shot or short drive. Player 5 moves to the block to set a screen if necessary.

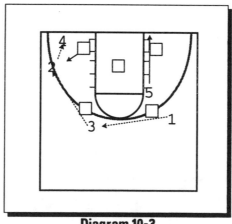

Diagram 10-3

Diagram 10-4: If nothing develops on the left side, quick ball reversal and a cut by 2 using a screen by 5 may create a scoring opportunity in the right corner or the low-post. As the ball swings from 2 to 3, 2 cuts and 4 fills the vacated spot for a jump shot or drive. Meanwhile, 5 sets a screen on the rear of the zone for 2. After screening, 5 can post-up in the lane for a pass from 1 or 2. If the back-line defender anticipates and fights the screen by 5, 1 and 5 can read the situation, with 1 faking a pass to 2, then hitting 5 coming up the lane.

NOTE: Against teams that key and overplay a scorer on one side of the court, Red uses quick ball and player movement to create a scoring opportunity on the other side. On 2's initial cut to the left side, he is looking for a two-on-one opportunity. On 2's return to the right side, he uses a screen to create a scoring opportunity.

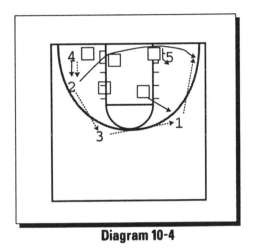

Diagram 10-4

Diagrams 10-5 through 10-7 show Red against a 1-2-2 zone. Diagrams 10-8 through 10-10 illustrate Red against a 1-3-1 zone.

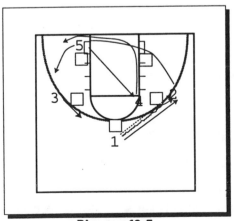

Diagram 10-5

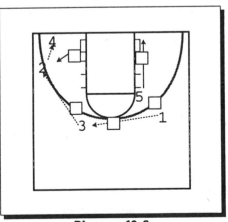

Diagram 10-6

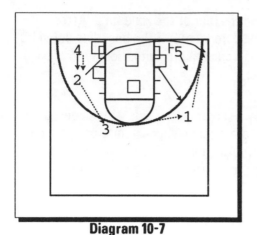

Diagram 10-7

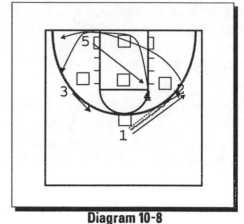

Diagram 10-8

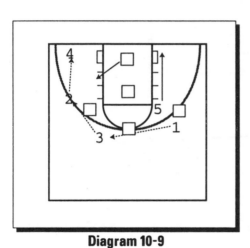

Diagram 10-9

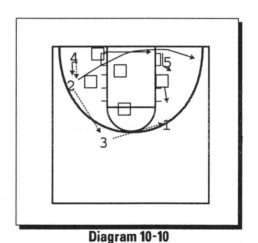

Diagram 10-10

Drills for Red

In diagram 10-11, we drill just the second part of Red. The first part involves hard cuts and ball reversal. However, the second part involves screening for a jump shot by 2 and feeding the pivot from the 1 or 2 position. We put two defenders on the court to play the screen and deny scoring opportunities for 2 and 5.

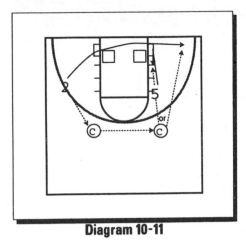

Diagram 10-11

Diagrams of Set Plays: Fade

Diagram 10-12: The initiation of the quick-hitting Red Series play called Fade against a 1-2-2 defense, is shown.

Player 1 initiates the play off a pass or dribble with 2. Player 2 cuts behind the defense and hides for a moment as 1 prepares to reverse the ball to 3. Meanwhile, 4 moves down the lane to set a screen on the rear player in the zone.

Diagram 10-13: Player 5 comes up the lane and will have a scoring opportunity if the zone neglects him. Player 1 passes to 3. On a quick ball reversal to 1, 2 uses the screen set by 4. Scoring opportunities occur according to how the defense reacts. The options are a fake pass to 2 and a look for 5 coming up the lane, or a pass to 2, who can take a jump shot or feed 4 in the low-post.

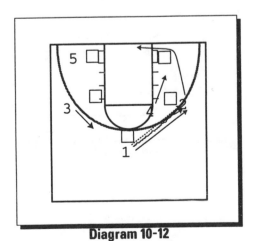

Diagram 10-12

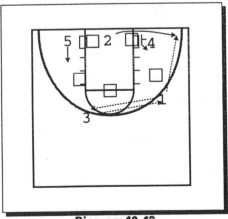

Diagram 10-13

Diagrams 10-14 and 10-15 show Fade against a 1-3-1 defense.

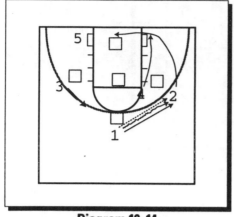

Diagram 10-14

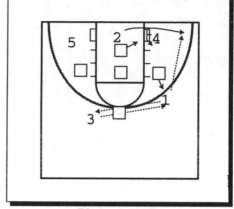

Diagram 10-15

Drills for Fade

• Diagram 10-16: A coach or manager sends 2 on a cut to the basket area. On a pass to another coach or manager, 4 sets a screen on the back of the zone.

• Diagram 10-17: On ball reversal back to the coach simulating 1, 2 practices using the screen and explores the possibilities of passing to 4 in the low-post.

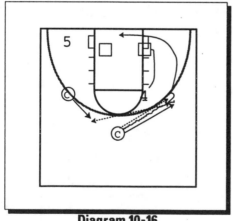

Diagram 10-16

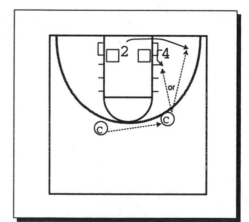

Diagram 10-17

Diagrams Of Set Plays: Middle

Diagram 10-18: Let's start by showing Middle against a 1-2-2 defense. Initiate the play as if you expect quick movement by 2 and 4 to the opposite side of the court for a possible two-on-one situation. Player 4 cuts behind the defense and hides for a moment.

Diagram 10-19: Instead of 4 continuing to the short corner, he comes up the lane for a possible scoring opportunity on a pass from 3. This play is especially effective once 4 has gone to the short corner once or twice, and if the middle of the defense is vulnerable, as in a 1-2-2 zone or some 2-3 zones.

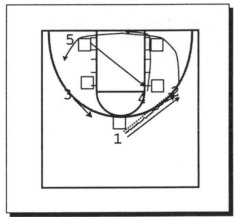
Diagram 10-18

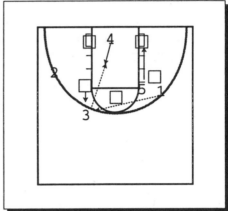
Diagram 10-19

Diagrams 10-20 and 10-21 show Middle against a 2-3 defense.

NOTE: Since the play doesn't employ screens and is a quick hitter, we don't drill it in practice.

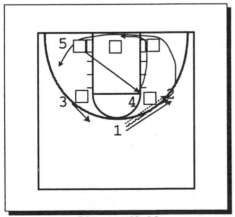
Diagram 10-20

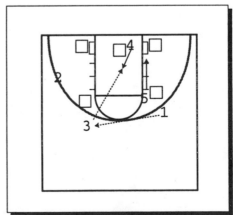
Diagram 10-21

Diagrams of Set Plays: Comeback

You've run the initial phase of the Red Series, trying to create scoring opportunities for 5, 4, or 2. Perhaps a variation can catch the defense by surprise. Diagrams 10-22 and 10-23 show the variation we call Comeback against a 1-2-2 defense.

Diagram 10-22: You've worked 2 off a screen by 4. As the ball is reversed from 2 to 3 to 1, 2 cuts behind the defense as if he is going to the opposite side of the court to use a screen by 5.

Diagram 10-23: Rather than filling the spot vacated by 2, 4 screens the rear of the zone on his side. Player 5 comes up the lane for a possible feed from 1. The ball is reversed back to 3. Player 3 can pass to 2, who uses a screen for a jump shot or feeds the screener, 4. Players 3 and 4 have the option of reading the defense. If the rear defender anticipates and fights through the screen to get to 2 in the corner, 3 can fake a pass to the corner and look for 4 coming up the lane for a scoring opportunity.

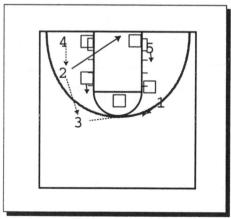

Diagram 10-22

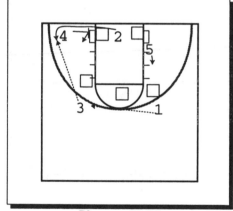

Diagram 10-23

Diagrams 10-24 and 10-25 show Comeback against a 1-3-1 defense.

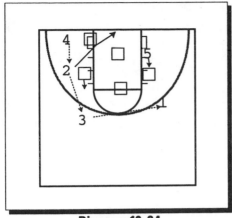

Diagram 10-24

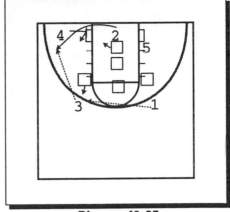

Diagram 10-25

Drills for Comeback

• Diagram 10-26: This drill employs two offensive players, two defensive players, and two coaches or managers. Work the second phase of the Comeback to improve timing and screening and to create scoring opportunities.

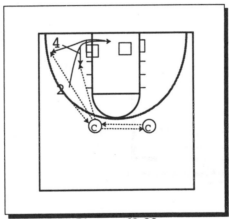

Diagram 10-26

Diagrams of Set Plays: Go

Diagram 10-27: Initiate Red as usual, but instead of 4 moving behind the defense to the opposite short corner, he sets a diagonal downscreen for 5.

Diagram 10-28: On ball reversal from 1 to 3, 5 uses the screen on the rear of the zone for a scoring opportunity in the lane area. If 3 occupies a defender in the front of the zone, the pass to 5 may be available.

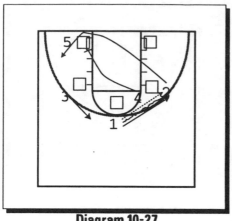

Diagram 10-27

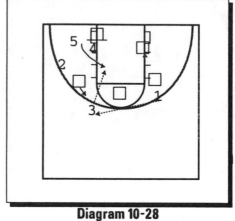

Diagram 10-28

Diagrams 10-29 and 10-30 show Go against a flat 2-3 defense.

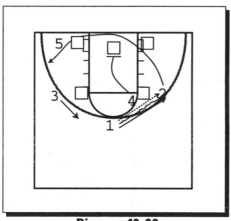

Diagram 10-29

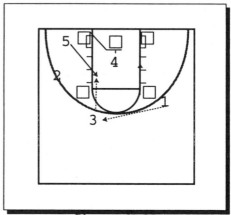

Diagram 10-30

Drills for Go

• Diagram 10-31: Using two coaches or a coach and a manager with two offensive players, work against one or two rear-zone defenders on the timing and use of the screen.

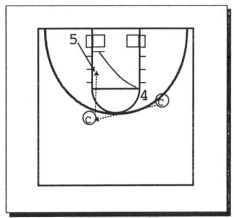

Diagram 10-31

Diagrams of Set Plays: Dribble Block

Diagram 10-32: In this movement series action you can easily switch 2 and 3 according to which player is better at using a screen off the dribble. The play is most effective against a two-guard-front zone, such as a 2-1-2 or a 2-3.

Player 1 initiates the play, sending 2 to the corner on the opposite side of the court. Player 4 rolls down the lane ballside. Player 5 comes straight up the lane for screening action.

Diagram 10-33: When the ball is reversed from 1 to 3, 3 uses a screen by 5 and dribbles into a gap area for an open jump shot. If the rear of the zone comes out to play him, 3 has several options. He can pass to 5 rolling to the basket for a scoring opportunity; he can take a return pass from 5 for a lay-up or post-up situation; he can pass to 2 for a jump shot. Player 4 is stationed in rebounding position on the opposite side.

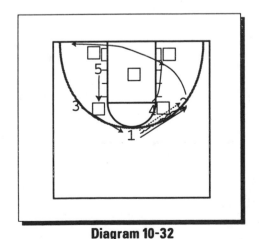

Diagram 10-32

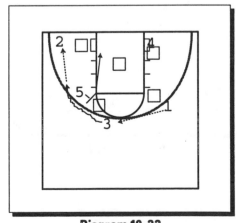

Diagram 10-33

Drills for Dribble Block
• Diagrams 10-34 and 10-35: A coach works with three offensive players: 2, 3, and 5. The defense consists of two or three players, one of whom should be the front player 5 is attempting to screen. The quick use of the screen and the timing of 2 and 5's roll are critical in creating three different scoring opportunities.

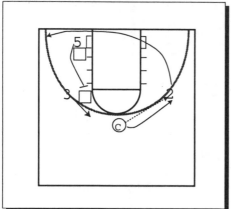

Diagram 10-34

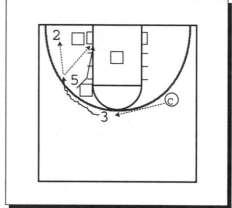

Diagram 10-35

Diagrams of Set Plays: Philly
This play is very effective play for a forward, 3, who can score with his back to the basket. Diagrams 10-36 and 10-37 show Philly against a 1-2-2 defense.

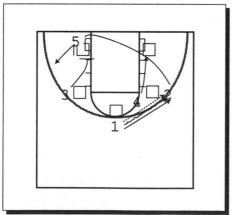

Diagram 10-36

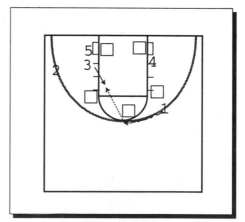

Diagram 10-37

Diagram 10-36: Begin with the usual movement by 1 and 2. Player 4 rolls down the lane on the ballside; 3 moves down the lane as if to set a double-screen with 5. Diagram 10-37: Player 1 dribbles hard left to occupy a defender on the front left side of the zone. Player 2 continues to a gap area created by a screen on the rear of the zone by 5. Player 4 is in rebounding position, and 1 has three options. He can pass to 3, button-hooking up the lane, to 2 for a jump shot, or to 5, who is open in the low-post after setting a screen. Player 1 may also be open for an alley-oop pass if the rear of the zone rushes out to cover 2 and 3. Diagrams 10-38 and 10-39 show Philly against a flat 2-3 defense.

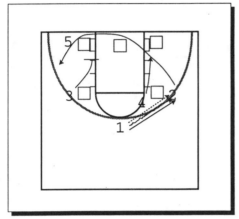

Diagram 10-38

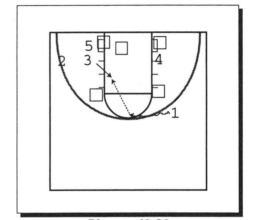

Diagram 10-39

Drill for Philly

• Diagrams 10-40 and 10-41: With a coach and players 2, 3, and 5, you can simulate the action of this play against two or three defenders.

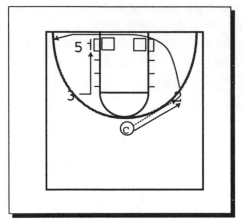

Diagram 10-40

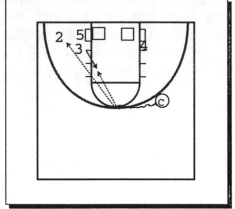

Diagram 10-41

CHAPTER 11

Set Plays: Attacking From the Rear

Go back to Chapter 1 of this book and you'll find a section on the basic principle and approach for attacking zone defenses. The premise is simple: what your opponents don't see can hurt them. So why not take advantage of an opponent's zone defense with a handful of set plays designed to attack from the rear? We have three such plays: "South Carolina, Away, and Away 3." Each play uses interior screens and a lob pass to produce a high-percentage scoring opportunity.

The benefits are obvious. First, by attacking along the baseline or from the weak side you create yet another problem for a zone defense which already may be stretched to its limit. Second, you create opportunities for high-flying interior players to do their thing, creating offensive balance in the process. And third, the resulting slam dunks and easy baskets can be extremely demoralizing to an opponent and invigorating for your team.

To run these plays successfully you must have the following three weapons in your arsenal: a ballhandler/passer who can deliver an accurate lob pass; an interior screener who understands how to set timely and legal screens; and a high-flying finisher who can convert the lob pass into a basket. Note here that your finisher need not be a dunking demon. The "catch-and-finish" aspect of these plays can take place below the rim.

South Carolina
South Carolina is a special play that has a completely different look than the Red Series. We use this play against 1-3-1 defenses, which are particularly vulnerable to alley-oop passes. It may also be effective against high 1-2-2 or 2-3 defenses.

Diagram 11-1: Player 2 dribbles to the left to occupy the left-wing defender in a 1-3-1 zone.

Diagram 11-2: On ball reversal to 1, 3 cuts diagonally to the right block to occupy the rear defender in a 1-3-1 zone. Meanwhile, 5 sets a backpick on the wing of the zone to create an alley-oop opening for 4 on the left-block.

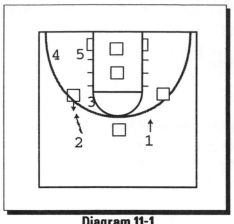

Diagram 11-1

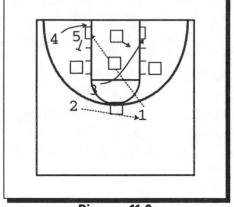

Diagram 11-2

Diagrams 11-3 and 11-4 show the same action against a 1-2-2 defense. Diagrams 11-5 and 11-6 show South Carolina against a 2-3 defense.

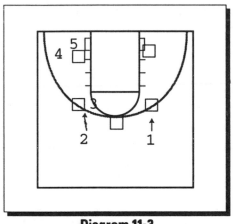

Diagram 11-3

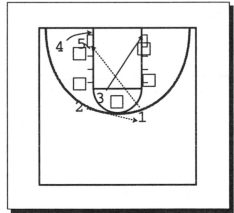

Diagram 11-4

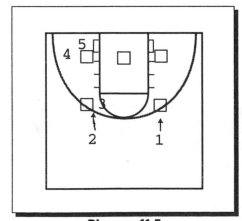

Diagram 11-5

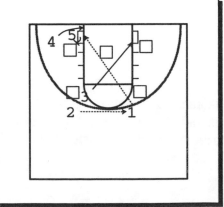

Diagram 11-6

NOTE: You can switch 1 and 2 according to which player throws the better alley-oop pass. You obviously want your best leaper on the left-block to receive the alley-oop pass. As you can see, switching roles according to skills is easily accomplished in this quick-hitting play.

Away and Away 3

Since the first edition of this book appeared in 1989, we have added two lob plays to our zone attack. These plays, Away and Away 3, diversified our attack and added an element of confusion for defenders. As you'll see, these plays originate in much the same way, but produce different finishes. This creates problems for defenders, who not only must be aware of what is happening behind them, but now face the very real problem of responding to multiple threats.

Away employs a screen by 5 against the middle of the zone to free 4 for a lob pass and score. Diagrams 11-7 and 11-8 detail the initiation and finish of Away against a 2-3 defense.

In Diagram 11-7, 1 initiates the offense by passing to 3 and cutting to the opposite side of the floor. 4 and 5 exchange places on the low blocks. 2 moves to the top of the key for a pass from 3.

In Diagram 11-8, 2 passes to 1. 3 screens for 2, who fades to an opening on the right wing. 5 screens the middle defender, while 4 moves across the floor and pins the weakside baseline defender away from the basket. 1 has the option of a lob pass to 4 or a skip pass to 2 for an open shot from the wing.

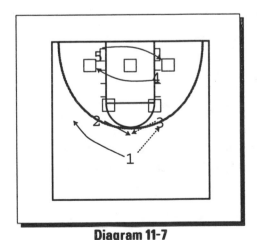

Diagram 11-7

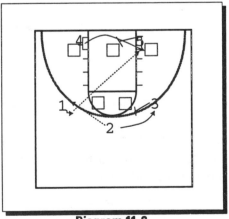

Diagram 11-8

There are several keys to this play. 1 must be a capable passer with the judgement to skip the ball to 2 if the lob pass isn't open. 4 must be strong enough to pin an interior defender away from the basket, catch a lob pass, and finish with authority. 5 must make a quick, legal screen, then clear the lane before being whistled for a 3-second violation. 2 makes the play more effective by posing a legitimate threat from the wing.

Away 3 is a variation of the same play. Instead of a lob pass to 4 being the first option, Away 3 creates an opening for the 3 man to cut from the wing for a lob pass. This variation creates difficult decisions for weakside defenders, especially if they have already seen Away.

Initiate this offense the same way you initiated Away (Diagram 11-7). In Diagram 11-9, 1 has received the pass from 2. 5 screens the middle defender. 4 loops behind the defense to screen the weakside defender. 3 cuts behind the two screeners to receive a lob pass from 1.

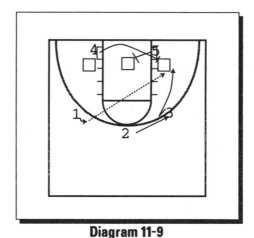

Diagram 11-9

Consider the problems the defense faces here. Both the middle and weakside interior defenders are being screened from behind. If the weakside baseline defender has already been pinned away from the basket on Away, he may fight to take away what he believes is a potential lob to 4. In so doing, he takes himself out of position to defend against a lob to 3.

CHAPTER 12

Three-Point Shots: Zone-Busters

When the first edition of this book appeared in 1989, the three-point shot was a relatively new phenomenon at the college and high school levels of competition. Even so, after only a few years of experimentation it was obvious to most observers that a makeable three-point shot altered the fundamental mathematics and strategies of basketball. Changes in coaching philosophy quickly followed.

Coaches who employed conservative zone defenses designed to force perimeter jump shots considered switching to aggressive matchup zones or man-to-man, and with good reason. In conjunction with a shot clock, the three-point shot enables teams to rally from seemingly insurmountable deficits. Even at the high school level, with fewer great shooters and no shot clock, the size of the so-called "safe" lead has increased dramatically. The areas a zone defense must cover have changed. Such critical statistics as shooting percentage and points-per-possession have been skewed. Think of it this way. Hitting 40 percent of your three-point attempts is equivalent to hitting 60 percent of your two-pointers.

If it isn't a whole new ballgame, it's certainly a different game, as the following examples demonstrate. Game one of the 1995 National Basketball Association championship series between the Houston Rockets and the Orlando Magic yielded game, team, and individual records for three-point shooting. The teams combined to attempt 62 three-pointers. The Rockets, who were 14-of-32 from three-point range, set marks for three-pointers attempted and made by one team. Houston guard Kenny Smith alone made seven threes, an NBA Finals record. One year later, the Rockets were again involved in a record-setting NBA playoff game with regard to three-point shots—this time on the losing side. The Seattle Sonics made 20 of 27 three-point shot attempts in their second round, second game victory over the soon-to-be-deposed defending NBA champions. What makes these examples even more startling is that NBA teams are required, by rule, to play man-to-man defense, which should limit three-point attempts and percentage. Imagine what your team can do against zone defenses, which in many cases concede three-point shots.

At the college level, where zone defense is allowed, Coach Rick Pitino's University of Kentucky Wildcats are among the more visible and effective proponents of the three-point shot. The Wildcats use the three-pointer as the high-octane fuel for a point-scoring machine. During the 1995-96 season when it won the NCAA championship, Kentucky attempted 573 three-point shots, hitting 222 for a .387 shooting percentage. During their relentless march in the 1996 tournament to the

NCAA title, the Wildcats were even more accurate from three-point range—making 44 of 97 attempts (a .454 percentage).

Eight years earlier the Final Four field included two teams—Nevada-Las Vegas and Providence—that never would have made it that far without the three-pointer. UNLV used the bomb to rally from an 18-point deficit in a tournament victory over Iowa. Providence, the tournament's dark horse, rode the three-point shooting skills of guards Billy Donovan and Delray Brooks all the way to the Final Four.

The effect of the three-pointer didn't stop there. As you may recall, Indiana won the NCAA title game in large part due to the three-point shooting skills of guard Steve Alford. Hitting seven three-pointers to Syracuse's four, Indiana defeated the Orangemen, 74-73. Without the three-pointer, Indiana would have lost, 69-67. Ironically, Indiana coach Bob Knight was one of the more vocal opponents of the three-pointer before it was installed nationwide.

High school coaches should understand that the three-point shot can affect their teams just as much, even if prep-level players aren't generally the type of shooters you see at the college level. During the 1986-87 season, for example, the Palmer (Iowa) High School team made 210 of 396 three-point attempts—a whopping 53-percent accuracy figure. I know a lot of college coaches who would take that kind of shooting anytime.

My first experience with the three-point shot came during the early 1970s, when I spent three seasons as assistant coach of the American Basketball Association's New York Nets. In the battle for the entertainment dollar the ABA pioneered the three-point shot with some occasionally wild results. A new role, "three-point specialist," was created and filled by such long-range ABA bombers as Rick Mount, Fred Lewis, Darrell Carrier, Lou Dampier, and Bob Verga. For the Nets, Rick Barry once hit seven three pointers in a row, and John Roche won several games, including a pivotal playoff game against the Kentucky Colonels, with his long-range bombs. And they truly were bombs. By comparison, the 19-foot, 9-inch three-pointer used at the college and high school levels is a very makeable shot. So why not use it?

Three-point opportunities abound within the framework of several continuities and set plays described earlier in this book, as well as our Flair Action and Motion offense options. All you have to do is match those opportunities to your better shooters, your "three-point specialists." If you have a player with a 17-to-21-foot shooting range, occasionally station him outside the three-point line. You'll see immediate and long-range strategic benefits.

A makeable three-point shot has altered the fundamental mathematics and strategies of basketball.

In the short term, your top shooters should be at a greater distance from defenders; therefore, they should have more time to shoot. Each shot carries a 50-percent higher return with a much smaller reduction in shooting percentage.

Over the long haul, by hitting a few three-pointers early in the game you'll probably force your opponent to switch out of the zone defense entirely, or at the very least, force your opponent to adjust to cover your perimeter shooters. This should open up gaps and passing lanes for your inside game. Also, by taking longer shots, you'll create longer rebounds and opportunities for putbacks.

Our offensive philosophy against zones offers three distinct advantages in creating three-point opportunities. First, screens free up three-point shooters. Second, the skip pass to the weak side offers immediate three-point opportunities. And third, good one-on-one players can take advantage of an overreacting defense to penetrate into gaps for attractive scoring opportunities.

Before examining these opportunities, let's lay some basic groundwork. It's obvious to me that zone defenses yield more three-point opportunities than do man-to-man defenses. Man-to-man defenses generally produce enough pressure on the player with the ball to force him to look to a teammate for the three-pointer. Against sagging or help-side man-to-man defenses, we can occasionally create a three-pointer by means of a skip pass or screen away from the ball. However, the angles at which offensive players come off screens often preclude the "catch around the ball" philosophy we prefer when receiving a pass on the perimeter. Fading potential shooters off backscreens or spotting up shooters can produce occasional three-point opportunities against man-to-man defenses. But again, all of this comes much more easily against zones.

It also is obvious to me that one true long-range threat often isn't enough to generate good three-point openings. Even in a zone, defenders find the single shooter and guard him closely, with and without the ball. A coach can actually hear this happening, as defenders shout the home-run threat's name or number to teammates whenever he spots up or comes off a pick. The best way to deal with this type of defense is to have two or three perimeter threats on the floor at the same time, especially when you need three-pointers and the other team is geared to stop them. With two or three legitimate shooting threats on the floor at once, it's virtually impossible for a zone defense to prevent high-percentage, uncontested, three-point shots.

Transition play also offers good three-point opportunities to the team willing to explore that possibility. Because the three-point shot has been a part of the international game for years, European players seem particularly comfortable with the idea of pulling up for three-pointers on the primary or secondary break.

Zone defenses are particularly vulnerable to this ploy due to two possible breakdowns. Should big players be slow in getting back to their assigned defensive positions, corner jump shots will be readily available. Should guards fall back to the basket in an attempt to cut off transition lay-ups, the key and wing areas are left wide open for guards or trailers to shoot the three-pointer. The same openings simply aren't as available when a team is playing man-to-man defense against a break.

As a coach, the ball's in your court. Know your personnel. Three-point shots are for three-point shooters, not for players who have trouble hitting 15-footers. Once you've determined which players can hit the three-pointer, give them two rules to shoot by. First, never look at your feet in relation to the three-point stripe after catching a pass. And second, never take a three-pointer with a defender draped all over you. The idea of incorporating the three-point shot into your regular zone attack is to increase your return without significantly decreasing your percentage. Looking at the floor or shooting while covered reduces your percentage.

As for the other team, recognize what defense it's playing and what type of shots will be available. The 2-3, 1-3-1, and 3-2 defenses present different opportunities. Use the right offense for the right shooter, and you'll have no trouble finding and taking advantage of those chances.

Creating Three-Point Shots

In the continuity Split, four players have the opportunity to take three-point shots. Diagram 12-1 shows the guards placed on either side of the top of the key and the forwards on either side of the court looking at the basket. By moving the ball quickly or by using the skip pass instead of using roll-and-replace action by the center and a forward, you'll find several wide-open three-pointers. Also, if one of your four perimeter players is able to penetrate the zone, thereby forcing defenders to react to him, he'll find teammates open for perimeter jump shots.

Continuity 13 (Diagram 12-2) offers three-point shots for the point guard down the middle or for the shooting guard and small forward on either wing. Again, by eliminating the center-forward roll-and-replace action, you create more three-point opportunities.

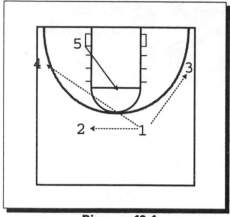

Diagram 12-1

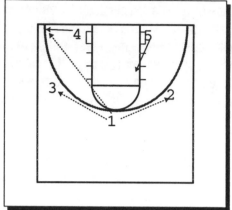

Diagram 12-2

The continuity Blue is a legitimate three-point weapon. Diagrams 12-3 and 12-4 show how the attacking team simply outnumbers defenders by quick guard movement from side to side. Shots will open up for the shooting guard on the wing or for the small forward in the corner. Also, a skip pass to the point guard creates three-point openings on the weak side.

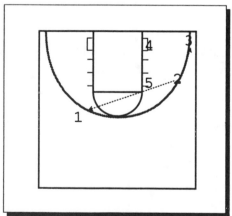

Diagram 12-3

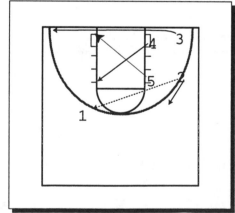

Diagram 12-4

The Gold attack (Diagram 12-5) is very effective if guards can pop from the corner. Screens give the shooters more time, and picks prevent back-line defenders from reacting quickly enough to stop the shot.

Special (Diagram 12-6) frees up guards and a forward in the corner for three-point shots.

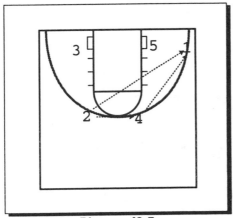

Diagram 12-5

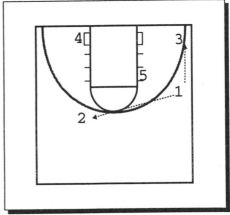

Diagram 12-6

In the Movement Series, we look to create three-point shots for our shooting guard. However, if the small forward has a hot hand, the two are readily interchangeable. The same flexibility that helps create two-point opportunities may be even more of a factor in three-point shot selection.

Red (Diagram 12-7) and its continuation create shots for the shooting guard as he rotates to the wing or back to the corner on the side he originated from.

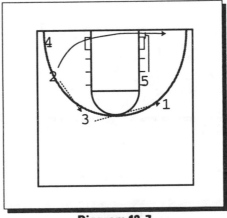

Diagram 12-7

Fade (Diagram 12-8) is a quick hitter with the help of a screen by the power forward.

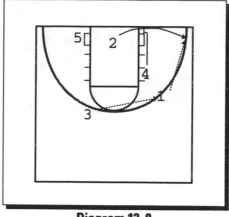
Diagram 12-8

Comeback and Dribble Block both create opportunities for the shooting guard.

Flare Action
Whether against odd-man or even-man front zones, Flare Action creates quick-hitting opportunities for good perimeter shooters.

Diagrams 12-9, 12-10, and 12-11 show Flare Action in detail. In Diagram 12-9 the offense is attacking a 2-3 or 2-1-2 zone. 1 initiates the play by passing to 3, who cuts from the foul line to the top of the key. On the flight of the pass from 1 to 3, 4 and 5 set screens against the perimeter defenders. 3 can pass to either 1 or 2 (presumably your best three-point shooters) who have "flared" to wing areas beyond the three-point arc.

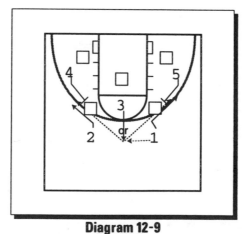
Diagram 12-9

Diagram 12-10 shows Flare Action against a 1-2-2 or 3-2 zone. Diagram 12-11 shows the same attack against a 1-3-1 zone defense.

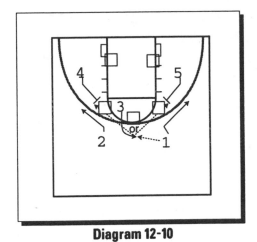

Diagram 12-10

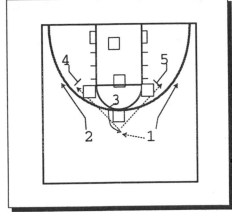

Diagram 12-11

Motion

As we've learned more about attacking zone defenses for three-point shots, we've discovered that many of the same opportunities a Motion offense creates against man-to-man defenses also are available against zones. Your team may already run Motion-style offense against man-to-man defense. Why not consider the same attack against zones?

We have found that four-out, one-in, or five-out motion attacks are particularly useful against matchup zones. Matchups typically employ many man-to-man defensive principles, so your zone attack must include sufficient ball and player movement to create three-point opportunities. Motion offense creates this type of movement, making it more difficult for zone defenders to match up against individual offensive players.

Four-out, one-in Motion offense features four perimeter players and one interior player. The perimeter players pass, move, cut, and screen, often to and from spots beyond the three-point line. Meanwhile the interior player flashes from block to block or to the high post, occasionally setting screens for perimeter players.

In five-out Motion, all five players use the perimeter skills of passing, moving, cutting, screening, and shooting, occasionally even posting up when the opportunity presents itself.

Diagrams 12-12 through 12-19 show some of the specific three-point shooting opportunities created by Motion offense against zone defense.

In Diagram 12-12 basic pass-and-screen-away action creates a quick three-point shot. 1 passes to 3, then sets a screen either against a defender matched up on 2 or against the defender responsible for the area on the left side of the key. 3 passes to 2 for a three-point shot.

Suppose the defense anticipates and eludes the screen to deny the three-point shot by 2. In Diagram 12-13, 1 reads this situation and pops off the screen to a spot beyond the three-point line. Instead of passing to 2, 3 skips the ball to 1 for a shot.

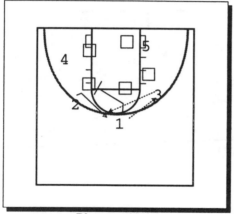

Diagram 12-12

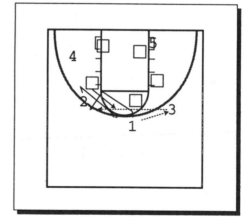

Diagram 12-13

In Diagram 12-14 the offense combines Motion and Flare Action principles to create a three-point shot. 1 passes to 2. 3 screens the defender matched up on 1 or the defender responsible for the area on the right side of the key. This frees 1 to accept a skip pass from 2 for a three-point shot.

Diagram 12-15 shows an option which becomes available should the defense take away the Flare Action opening for 1. After attempting to set a screen, 3 steps out beyond the three-point line for a pass from 2.

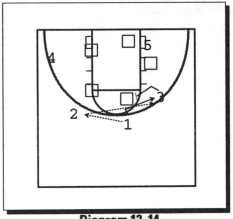

Diagram 12-14

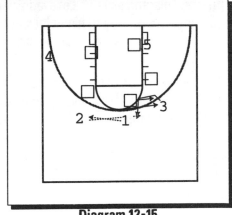

Diagram 12-15

Diagrams 12-16 and 12-17 show the effective use of a high block to create a quick-hitting three-point opportunity for a guard who can shoot off the dribble or a spot-up shooter. In Diagram 12-16, 3 sets a block for 1. To take maximum advantage of this opportunity, 1 must use his dribble to come shoulder-to-shoulder and hip-to-hip with the screener, 3. A three-point shot often results. Should the defender anticipate the block and overplay 1, 3 can step out to the top of the key for a pass from 1 and a high-percentage look at the basket (Diagram 12-17).

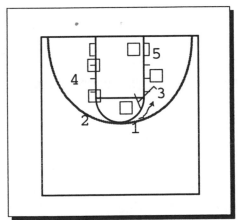

Diagram 12-16

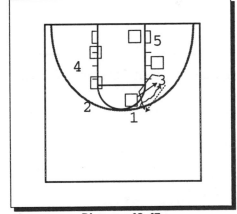

Diagram 12-17

In previous diagrams we've detailed some of the three-point options created by pass-and-screen-away or high-block action. Diagrams 12-18 and 12-19 show pass-and-cut action against zone defenses.

In Diagram 12-18 the offense is running four-out, one-in Motion. 1 passes to 2 and cuts to the basket. Assuming the immediate return pass is unavailable, 1 continues through the defense to spot in the corner. With the help of a screen by 5, 1 may be wide open for a three-point shot from the strong side. This type of movement by 1 is particularly effective because the defense cannot assume which way a cutter will move. In this case, 1 may go to either corner, creating equally good three-point openings.

Diagram 12-19 shows the pass-and-cut option with movement to the weak side. Once again, 1 passes to 2 and cuts to the basket. Should the zone defense match up quickly to take away threats by 3 and 4, quick ball reversal or a skip pass from 2 will result in an open three-point shot for 1.

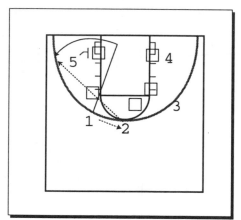

Diagram 12-18

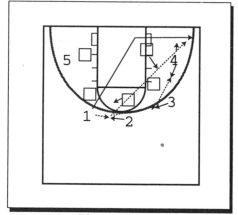

Diagram 12-19

Time and Score

If crunch time arrives and you're behind, the three-point shot, even the mere threat of a three-pointer, can help get you back in the game. Don't start your three-point attack too soon, as you can shoot yourself right out of the game. Instead, look for the happy medium—the time and score situation in which you can take unforced three pointers, or if need be, accept easy two-pointers against an overreacting defense.

Remember, whichever offense you choose isn't necessarily limited to three-point shots. You still have attractive two-point options, especially if the defense is playing to cut off three pointers. Sometimes it's easier to score three loosely defended two pointers than to get off two tough, well-covered three-pointers. The effect—six quick points—is the same.

When it gets down to do or die, certain continuities and set plays create three-point shots more quickly than others. Split, 13, Blue, and Special can get you a quick three-pointer after just one pass. Gold requires two or three passes, while Movement Series plays may require as many as four passes before a three-pointer is available. Given those constraints, it's obvious that you don't call certain plays with limited time remaining.

With the shot or game clock below ten seconds, we have found that a quick Split or 13 assures us a good three-point opening. The Gold continuity has been successful for us in getting three-point shots from the corner with more than ten seconds remaining. The addition of an effective screen gives the shooter more time to select and take the shot he wants.

Should the defense jump out to the shooter before the pass can be made, we look for double duck-in action (Diagram 12-20) for a quick score inside, followed by an immediate timeout or foul. If the defense chooses a man-to-man alignment, we stay with the Gold play but give the shooter a double-screen for the shot (Diagram 12-21).

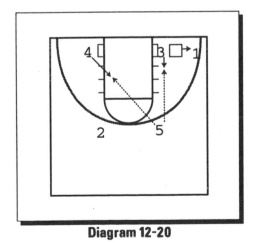

Diagram 12-20

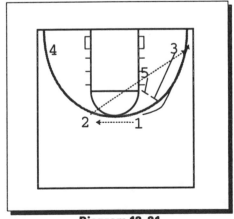

Diagram 12-21

CHAPTER 13

Inbounds Plays

Inbounding the Ball on the Baseline

Throughout his career, whether as coach of the NCAA champion Marquette Warriors or as a network television commentator, Al McGuire has advocated zone defense on baseline inbounds situations. McGuire believes that man-to-man defense is particularly vulnerable to the quick screens and passes teams use when inbounding the ball.

Coaches at all levels of competition generally agree with this philosophy. Many predictably align their teams in 2-3 zone defenses against inbounding opponents. Even when the zone isn't a 2-3 it effectively takes on a 2-3 look to defend key areas along the baseline.

These baseline inbounding situations represent a real opportunity for the offensive team. Our system of screens, player movement, and quick passes takes advantage of zone defenses' inherent weaknesses. Here's what I mean.

First and foremost, thanks to a stoppage in play, the attacking team can catch its breath, check time and score, decide which play to call, then initiate from a spot on the floor a mere 10 or 12 feet from the basket. There's no need to dribble up the floor against pressure just to initiate an attack. Nor must we count on the point guard to initiate the offense. In a sense we've penetrated to a vulnerable area in the defense. From there we can use any player, tall or small, to inbound the ball. These factors give us an immediate advantage.

We know that most teams playing zone defense under the basket will line up with three tall players (forwards and center) guarding the baseline and two small players (guards) in the paint. This enables us to attack weak players and areas, often creating the kind of mismatches that result in easy baskets.

Think of it from the defenders' perspective. Playing zone defense against a team inbounding under the basket presents fundamental problems. The opponent starts the play from an ideal position with a multitude of options. Given where the play is initiated, the "ball-you-man" principle of defensive basketball takes a real beating. Often defenders don't realize they've been beaten until the ball is in the basket. By then it's too late for teammates, who have their own assignments, to offer help.

Given all of these factors, you'd think more coaches would consider man-to-man defense in these situations. Indeed, some do. But for the most part you still see a lot of zone defense played against teams inbounding the ball on the baseline. So why not gain an edge and be ready to attack when the opportunity presents itself?

Conveniently and effectively, we have adapted five of our set plays and one of our continuities for use in inbounding situations. Middle, Fade, and Philly from the Red Series (Chapter 10), Away 3 and Away (Chapter 11) and the continuity BC (Chapter 6) are effective weapons when inbounding the ball against zone defenses. One benefit to you as a coach is that you won't be forced to "reinvent the wheel" to inbound the ball. You'll be able to call plays your team already uses in halfcourt situations. When teaching time is short this kind of "two-fer" is a real plus.

In this chapter I'll also detail several other quick-hitting plays for use when inbounding against zone defenses. In our system all of these plays begin with the inbounder slapping the ball then passing it. Cuts, screens and outlets occur on the flight of the pass.

Middle

Like its Red Series namesake, Middle creates an opportunity for your inside players, 4 and 5, to exploit openings in the gut of a 2-3 zone. Diagrams 13-1 and 13-2 show Middle and the options it offers to a smart, well-schooled team.

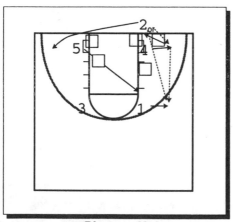

Diagram 13-1

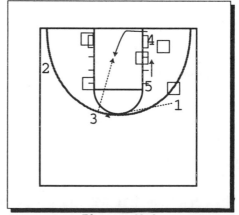

Diagram 13-2

When running Middle in a halfcourt setting, 2 cuts through the defense from the right wing to the opposite side of the court, and 4 loops from the foul line down the

Baseline inbounding situations represent a real scoring opportunity for the offensive team.

lane, then back up into an opening in the middle of the defense. For the inbounding variation of Middle, 2 inbounds the ball to 4 or 1, then clears to the opposite side of the court. The center, 5, moves from the weakside low post to the ballside high post.

If he receives the inbound pass, 4 passes the ball outside to 1, then follows 2 toward the opposite side of the court. If 2 passes directly to 1, 4 simply follows 2. The first look for 1 is to the ballside high post, where 5 may find an opening. If the middle defender in the zone responds to 5, 1 passes across the key to 3, who has a better angle for a quick pass to 4 attacking a vacant area in the defense.

Fade
When running Fade in a regular halfcourt setting you produce excellent opportunities for 2 to shoot an open jumper or feed a big man inside. The inbounds Fade offers many of the same opportunities and options.

Diagrams 13-3, 13-4, and 13-5 show the movement and options of Fade from an inbounding position. In Diagram 13-3, 2 inbounds the ball to 1 or 4, who quickly moves it to 1. In Diagram 13-4, 4 then sets a screen against the wing of the zone, freeing up 2 to step inbounds for a quick jump shot on the return pass from 1.

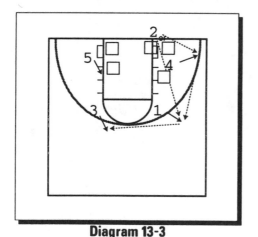

Diagram 13-3

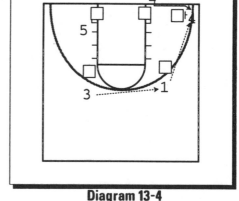

Diagram 13-4

While the quick-hitting play for 2 is an attractive option, it is by no means the only opening created by Fade. Diagram 13-3 shows that on a pass from 1 to 3, 5 may be open for a quick post-up or flashing move. The pass from 1 to 3 also effectively "moves" the zone to that side of the floor, creating even better openings for 2 and 4 on what has become the weak side of the floor. Should 3 pass back to 1, plays open up for both 2 and 4. 2 may be open in the corner. Meanwhile, should the defense overreact to the threat of 2, 4 may find an opening in the post area for a pass from 1 (Diagram 13-5).

1, 2, and 4 create an effective triangle, overloading one side of the zone defense and forcing defenders to make difficult decisions.

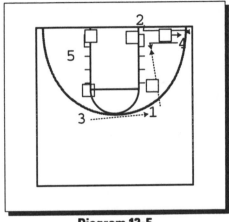

Diagram 13-5

Philly
While Middle and Fade create excellent opportunities for 2, 4, and 5, Philly is a great play for 3. After two or three quick passes, 3 will have the ball in his hands for a scoring opportunity in the paint.

In Diagram 13-6, 2 inbounds the ball to 4 or 1, then moves to the opposite corner or wing area. Whether on a pass from 4 or a direct pass from 2, 1 eventually receives the ball. Diagram 13-7 shows 1 dribbling toward the top of the key, while 5 and 3 move to set a screen in the low block area. 3 then hooks back to a gap in the middle of the zone.

1 has two options. He can pass the ball to 3 for a quick, high-percentage opportunity in the paint, or move it to 2 for a jump shot on the wing. Should the defense overreact, 2 may find 5 open for an alley-oop pass from the wing.

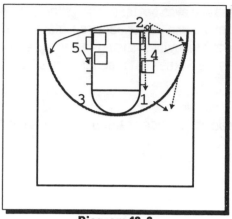

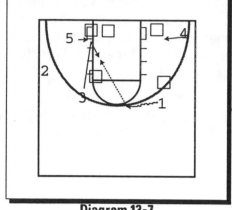

Diagram 13-6　　　　　　　　**Diagram 13-7**

Away 3 and Away

These two plays employ the same screening and passing action as their namesakes detailed in Chapter 11. The intent of each play is to create an opening for a lob pass and high-percentage inside opportunity. As its name implies, Away 3 is a set play for 3 to score. Away creates an opening for 4. Both plays employ a basic principle—attacking from the rear—to defeat a zone defense.

Diagrams 13-8 and 13-9 detail the inbounding version of Away 3. In Diagram 13-8, 2 inbounds the ball to 3 and moves under the basket to the opposite side of the floor. On the pass from 3 to 1 (Diagram 13-9), 4 and 5 set screens against baseline defenders. 5 screens the middle defender, preventing him from denying a lob pass. 4 moves across the baseline to screen the rear of the zone. This opens up a lob pass from 1 to 3. Note here that 5 must set his screen then quickly vacate the lane to avoid a 3-second violation.

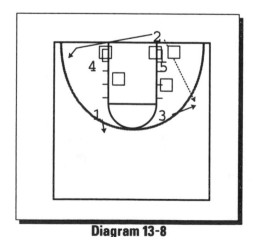

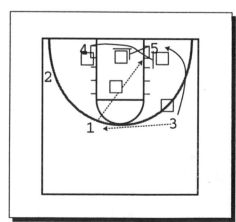

Diagram 13-8　　　　　　　　**Diagram 13-9**

Diagram 13-10 shows another lob play, Away, as run from a position on the baseline. The inbounding action is fundamentally the same as detailed in Diagram 13-8. On this play, however, 4 pins the rear baseline defender away from the basket, establishing perfect position for a lob pass from 1.

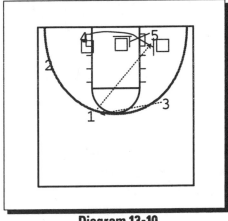

Diagram 13-10

BC

You will recall from Chapter 6 that BC is one of our continuities — not a "set play" such as Middle, Fade, and Philly. For this reason, BC may not be the kind of "quick hitting" play you'd use to inbound the ball with limited time on the shot or game clock. However, BC will free up inside players for high-percentage opportunities, and can be "continued" from one side of the court to the other until a scoring opportunity opens up.

When using BC in a halfcourt setting, 1 initiates the play by dribbling to 2's side of the floor. When inbounding the ball (Diagram 13-11), 1 initiates by passing the ball to 2 then clearing under the basket to the opposite side of the floor. Should 2 be overplayed, 3 serves as an outlet.

On 1's pass to 2, 5 screens the middle defender in the zone, creating an opening for 4, who loops on the baseline side from the opposite block to the ballside short corner. 5 then spins back to an opening in the mid-post area, while 3 moves to the opposite block for rebounding position.

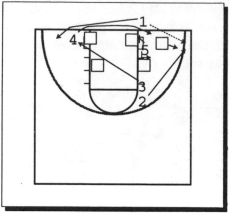

Diagram 13-11

Diagram 13-12 shows the continuation of BC with a pass from 2 to 1. On the pass, 4 and 3 "x-out." 4 flashes to the top-of-the-key area, then 3 flashes into a vacant area created with the help of a quick downscreen by 5. This action puts the defense in a difficult position. Presumably, the two perimeter defenders play 1 and 4 honestly. Meanwhile, with 5 screening a middle defender, there should be plenty of room for 3 to operate in the middle of the zone. If the baseline defender on 2's side moves to take away 3's opening, 2 may have an uncontested jump shot.

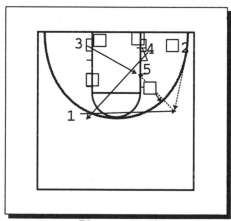

Diagram 13-12

BC may be continued to the opposite side of the court as detailed in Chapter 6.

Inbounding Options

Depending on your personnel and other considerations, you may prefer to attack zone defenses in a variety of ways other than those detailed previously in this chapter. Here's a group of quick-hitting inbounding plays, all of which rely on the basic principles we've outlined elsewhere in this book. These include quick ball and player movement and attacking the zone from the rear.

Diagram 13-13 shows a screening play that opens the gut of the zone. 3 inbounds to 2. On the pass from 2 to 1, 5 downscreens the defender responsible for the middle of the zone and covering the inbounder. 1 looks to 3 for the turnaround jump shot or move to the hoop.

Diagram 13-14 shows a play which may prove especially effective for teams blessed with two good perimeter shooters. 3 inbounds the ball. 4 screens a guard on the strong side for a wing jump shot by 1. 5 screens the back of the zone on the weak side for a jump shot by 2.

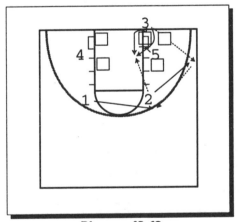

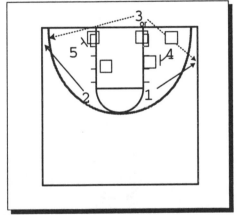

| Diagram 13-13 | Diagram 13-14 |

Diagram 13-15 is a quick-hitting play that surprises the zone defense and often yields an excellent inside opportunity. We've found this play especially valuable when the shot or game clock demands a quick shot, but it can be useful throughout the game. 1 inbounds the ball. He has two excellent options. 5 screens the middle defender, opening up a potential lob for 4. Should the weakside defender move to cover 4, he leaves 2 open for a baseline jump shot. In either case—a pass to 4 or to 2—the result should be a quick shot, often in no more than the time it takes for the pass recipient to catch and shoot.

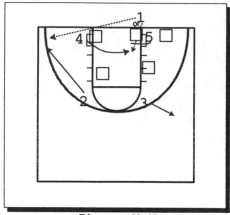

Diagram 13-15

Diagram 13-16 outlines a variation of the play shown in Diagram 13-15. On this play the inbounder, 1, lobs directly to 5 or passes in the corner to 2. 4 screens the weak side of the zone to create the opening for 2.

In Diagram 13-17 the objective is a quick 3-point shot, preferably for 2, but possibly for 3. Key screens are set by 4 and 5 to create an opening on the weak side of the zone for 2. 3 simultaneously spots up on the strong side.

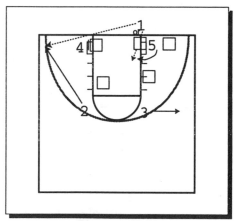

Diagram 13-16

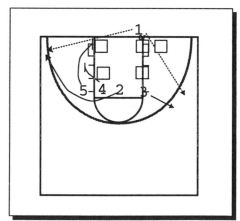

Diagram 13-17

"The zone defense concedes a variety of benefits to a patient, well-schooled offense."

—John Kresse

About the Authors

John Kresse

John Kresse is the head men's basketball coach and director of athletics at the College of Charleston. During Kresse's first 16 seasons at the College of Charleston his teams compiled a 387-105 record, including 24-4 and 23-6 records in 1994 and 1995. The College of Charleston received an at-large bid to the NCAA Tournament in 1994, and played in the post-season National Invitation Tournament in 1995. Earlier in Kresse's tenure, the College of Charleston won the NAIA championship in 1983 and placed third in 1988. From 1960 through 1979 Kresse played for and coached with Joe Lapchick and Lou Carnesecca at St. John's University and with the New York Nets in the American Basketball Association.

Richard Jablonski

Richard Jablonski is a research associate at the Medical University of South Carolina. From 1979 through 1988, he was a sports reporter and columnist for several newspapers. His coverage of College of Charleston basketball in 1983 earned first-place honors from the South Carolina Press Association. From 1988 through 1993; Jablonski served as the color commentator and play-by-play voice on the College of Charleston Radio Network.

ADDITIONAL BASKETBALL RESOURCES FROM